Interest Rate Cycles

An Introduction

Brian Romanchuk

Published by BondEconomics, Canada

www.BondEconomics.com

Published by BondEconomics, 2016, Montréal, Québec.

Nothing in this book constitutes investment or tax advice. Investors are advised to seek professional advice tailored to their situation. Although best efforts have been made to ensure the validity of information contained herein, there is no guarantee of its accuracy or completeness.

Library and Archives Canada
Interest Rate Cycles: An Introduction
Brian Romanchuk 1968-
ISBN 978-0-9947480-3-4 Epub Edition
ISBN 978-0-9947480-2-7 Kindle Edition
ISBN 978-0-9947480-4-1 Paperback Edition

Contents

Chapter 1 Overview

1.1 Introduction

This report offers an informal introduction to modern central bank watching, explaining why interest rates are raised and lowered across the business cycle. The objective is to illustrate the logic behind central bank decisions, without plunging into the mathematical complexity of modern monetary economic theory. Whenever possible, concepts are illustrated with charts of economic and financial time series.

Although the author is a follower of post-Keynesian economics, this text focuses on "mainstream" economic theory (sometimes called neoclassical economic theory). The explanation for this is that the central bankers who set the policy rate are followers of mainstream theory, and so we need to understand that theory if we wish to understand their decisions.

Therefore, if we want to understand why policy rates are administered the way that they are, we need to understand mainstream logic. One could imagine an alternative theory how interest rates *ought* to be set, but until central bankers adopt that theory, it tells us little about real world interest rate determination.

The underlying theme of the analysis is somewhat pessimistic. Mainstream macroeconomic theory is highly mathematical, and seems to offer a precise understanding of the business cycle. Unfortunately, at the core of the theory there are a number of variables that are not directly measured, and the current values of those variables are uncertain. It is easy to explain historical events, since estimates of those variables can be pinned down. However, the clarity of explanations for historical developments is in sharp contrast to the quality of model-based forecasts. The usefulness of the mainstream analytical framework is that it provides a way of thinking about the business cycle, at the cost of fundamental uncertainty around the values of key variables.

1.2 Post-World War II Interest Rate Trends

Economies in the developed world have behaved in a quite different fashion after World War II when compared to earlier eras. The Gold Standard constrained government finances as well as the accepted norms of policymaking behaviour. (In the *Gold Standard*, governments fixed the value of their currency relative to the price of gold.) The Great Depression and World War II upset the economic consensus, with central governments imposing command economies in order to pursue all-out military production. Governments loosened their control of the economy after World War II, but welfare state programs left governments much bigger when compared to pre-1930s norms.

Government finances also became less constrained. The Gold Standard gave way to the Bretton Woods system, whereby only foreign governments could convert their U.S. dollar holdings into gold. Since the United States had accumulated a significant proportion of the world's gold reserves by 1945, gold convertibility did not pose a significant constraint upon the U.S. government's actions. The fall in the ratio of gold reserves to the stock of U.S.

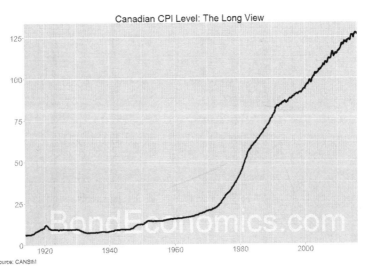

Canadian CPI Level: The Long View

Source: CANSIM

dollars in circulation put the Bretton Woods system into question by the mid-1960s, which eventually led President Nixon to abandon the Bretton Woods system in the early 1970s when the constraints finally began to bite into domestic policy options. The developed world (outside of continental Europe, which clings to currency pegging orthodoxy) moved to a system of free-floating "fiat" currencies. The subject of how a free-floating currency opens up the options for fiscal policy for a central government is the subject of an earlier report – *Understanding Government Finance*.

The previous chart shows one side effect of the change in the policy environment, using Canada as an example. Before World War II, the price level was tied to gold prices, and it was relatively stable. In the modern era, policies have favoured a policy of steady inflation. The price level profiles of other developed countries were generally similar to that of Canada. (As discussed in Section 3.3, Japan's inflation experience has been different.)

The rise in inflation was politically unpopular, and policies changed to bring it under control. The standard explanation is that "tight" monetary policy (that is, high interest rates) under Fed Chairman Volcker (which was echoed by other developed central banks) finally changed the trend of inflation. This caused the dramatic peaks in policy interest rates (the Fed Funds

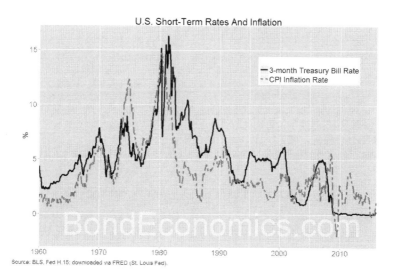

U.S. Short-Term Rates And Inflation

— 3-month Treasury Bill Rate
- - CPI Inflation Rate

Source: BLS, Fed H.15; downloaded via FRED (St. Louis Fed).

rate in the United States) in the early 1980s (previous chart).

This exaggerated rise in interest rates in the 1970s has since skewed views about the future path of interest rates. It is often described as a *supercycle*, as interest rates rose and fell during the business cycles, while following a general trend upward (until around 1980) and then lower. The focus of this report is the discussion of the cyclical movements of interest rates, without speculating upon the drivers of the supercycle.

In recent years, with the policy rate reaching 0% in many countries, the focus has moved towards "unorthodox" monetary policy measures – such as Quantitative Easing, negative interest rates, and even "helicopter money." This report largely avoids a discussion of these policies (although the effect of the zero bound on interest rates is discussed). One justification is that this text is introducing the framework for "orthodox" monetary policy measures, and that the unorthodox measures add too much complexity. The second justification is that the author believes that these unorthodox policies are largely ineffective, but the historical record is too short to justify that argument.

Finally, this report is focused on developed countries with free-floating currencies and control of their central bank ("currency sovereignty"). This includes countries such as Australia, Canada, Japan, Sweden, the United Kingdom, and the United States. These countries face no risk of *involuntary* default, as I discussed in my earlier report *Understanding Government Finance*. Conversely, although the euro floats versus other currencies, the constituent nations have fixed their currencies against each other, and involuntary governmental default is a very real risk. As for the so-called developing countries, the analysis herein may be broadly applicable, but these countries often have different preoccupations than the developed countries. For example, the value of the currency is emphasized much more by policymakers, even when the currency is notionally floating. For stylistic reasons, this currency sovereignty assumption is not repeated throughout the text, but many statements made herein rely upon that qualification.

The composition of the rest of this report is as follows.

- Chapter 2 provides an overview of the theoretical concepts used in discussing the business cycle. The bulk of the discussion uses mainstream concepts, tied together by the notion of a "Taylor Rule." However, Section 2.9 discusses how post-Keynesian analysis diverges from the mainstream in this area. Later chapters are much less theoretical in nature.
- Chapter 3 gives a brief overview of post-1990 monetary history. It focuses on the United States, although there is a brief discussion of other developed countries in Section 3.3.
- Chapter 4 discusses how various financial markets react to interest rates cycles. The focus is on interest rate markets, but currencies are also discussed in Section 4.6.
- Chapter 5 turns to the most difficult part of the business cycle to analyse – recessions. The argument made here is that the well-known inability of the consensus to forecast recessions is not just bad luck or incompetence. Instead, it is an inherent property of the business cycle.
- Chapter 6 provides some brief concluding remarks, asking whether interest cycles in the future will follow the patterns of recent history.
- The Appendix offers a somewhat technical discussion of how a chart showing a range of Taylor Rule outputs was constructed.

1.3 About this Report

This report is informal, and the use of equations was largely avoided (only a few elementary expressions appear). Whenever possible, ideas are illustrated using charts of economic data. The References section gives the bibliographic details (and hyperlinks) for materials that are cited. The objective of this report is to give a high-level overview of the subject, and not to act as a textbook.

Small changes have been made to this paperback edition relative to the eBook editions. These changes reflect format differences.

The text is aimed at readers who are comfortable reading financial news articles, and who wish to understand interest rate markets. Whenever possible, technical terms are defined, although it is assumed that the reader is familiar with basic concepts, such as the business cycle. However, these definitions are kept brief in order to avoid distracting more advanced readers. Furthermore, the text quite often refers to bond *bull* and *bear* markets. These terms can be confusing to readers not familiar with fixed income markets; bond yields move in the opposite direction of bond prices. That means that a bond bull market features falling yields (rising prices), and a bear market features rising yields. This means that yield charts have return connotations opposite to those of a stock price chart. From the perspective of stock investors, bond investors think backwards (and vice versa).

Sections of this report previously appeared as drafts on the website BondEconomics.com.

The report follows Canadian spelling and grammatical conventions. Like most things Canadian, it is a hybrid of English and American customs, and so readers on both sides of the Atlantic may find some unfamiliar usages.

Finally, the author would like to thank Judy Yelon for copy editing this report.

Montréal, Québec, Canada, May 14, 2016.

Chapter 2 Central Bank View of Policy Rates

2.1 Introduction

Central bankers administer the short-term interest rate; it is not set by market forces. As a result, how central bankers believe interest rates should be set is of utmost importance for analysis of the fixed income markets.

Although modern monetary economics is highly mathematical, it is hardly a settled science like physics or chemistry. Unfortunately, the key concepts in discussing the business cycle (such as the output gap, or the natural rate of interest) are not directly measured. As a result, many judgment calls end up being smuggled into the discussion via the back door.

The mathematical nature of modern mainstream monetary economics makes it difficult for those who are not mathematically inclined to delve into the theory. A non-mathematical explanation (such as given in this report) risks glossing over what the theory truly says. A verbal description risks not truly representing the properties of the mathematical model. One source for explanatory material would be introductory articles published by central banks. However, for readers who are mathematically proficient, one of the least complex introductions to mainstream monetary theory that I am acquainted with is *Monetary Policy, Inflation, and the Business Cycle: An Introduction to the New Keynesian Framework*, by Jordi Galí. (The book is intended for graduate economics students, so it does require a strong mathematics background to follow.)

This chapter focuses on these concepts, which are tied together into a single formula – a Taylor Rule. Although real world central banks do not blindly follow mathematical rules when setting the policy rate, analysts can use them to gauge the overall expected trend in interest rates.

Post-Keynesian economists are skeptical about the mainstream theory that is discussed in this chapter; it concludes with a brief discussion of some their criticisms.

Please note that this chapter holds the theoretical background used within this report. Readers who are not familiar with economic theory might consider skipping ahead to the later chapters, where the practical implications of this theory are discussed.

2.2 Inflation Targeting

The post-1990 policy environment has been dominated by several orthodox views – fiscal conservatism, free trade, labour market flexibility, and inflation-targeting central banks. This period has been characterised by low and stable inflation rates, for which central banks have rushed to take credit, courtesy of their inflation-targeting policies. It has also been characterised by asset bubbles, growing income inequality, and sluggish growth (branded as "secular stagnation"). Policymakers have been much less willing to take credit for those unwelcome developments.

The dissolution of the Bretton Woods fixed exchange rate system in the 1970s destroyed the analytical system that central banks worked with. Policymakers were uncomfortable with the lack of overriding principles for the day-to-day task of setting interest rates. By the early 1990s, a new framework had been embraced by academics and central bankers – inflation targeting. The main objective of the central bank is stabilising inflation near a target level; other considerations are of secondary importance. New Zealand was the first developed country to adopt inflation targeting in 1990. In most cases, the choice for the inflation target was 2%. The United States is one of the few holdouts without a formal target, as Congress has set a mixed policy target for the Federal Reserve ("maximum employment" and "stable prices"). The Federal

Reserve has *informally* adopted as a target a 2% inflation rate (as measured by the deflator for Personal Consumption Expenditures), its interpretation of the vague Congressional policy mandate.

The Financial Crisis shook the consensus about policymaking, as central banks rediscovered the need to regulate the financial system. Financial stability has to be worked into the mandate for central banks somehow. At the same time, it is unclear how this additional mandate relates to interest rate policy.

Looking at the period 2010-2015, economic growth was generally sluggish in the developed economies (closer to depression conditions in the euro area periphery). The orthodox view was that low real interest rates were needed to revive economic growth, to prevent inflation from dropping below target. At the same time, asset bubbles appeared to be forming. Hiking interest rates to dampen enthusiasm in the financial markets risked dropping economies back into recession before the damage from the Financial Crisis was fully healed.

The only palatable option appears to be that tighter regulation will address financial stability concerns, and interest rate policy will be used to manage inflation risk. This leaves us with a policy framework that is not greatly different from the previous inflation-targeting orthodoxy, except that central banks spend more time thinking about their lender-of-last-resort powers. Since those lending powers are needed infrequently, the factors determining interest rates will not greatly change. It remains to be seen whether the new regulatory environment will in fact reduce the potential for a financial crisis. Since the driver for financial crises is the state of private sector balance sheets, I have my doubts about the efficacy of regulatory steps taken so far. However, investors presumably learned at least some lessons from the Financial Crisis, and so they are unlikely to disregard liquidity management to the same extent that they did before 2007.

In summary, we can assume that the central bank's primary objective remains inflation targeting, but we cannot ignore financial stability concerns. How those concerns affect the outlook for interest rates is unclear.

2.3 Inflation Expectations

Within mainstream models, inflation expectations are the primary driver of inflation. Although this is a reasonable view, it faces an awkward problem: what causes inflation expectations to move? Instead of trying to develop models to explain inflation, we end up trying to develop models of the formation of inflation expectations. It is unclear whether we are further ahead.

The emphasis on inflation expectations is to a certain extent a historical accident. Old "Keynesian" models used *adaptive expectations* – inflation expectations were just the average of historical inflation. This measure was usually calculated by the use of an *exponential moving average*, as in the chart below. As can be seen, the adaptive expectations measure of inflation expectations follows actual inflation with a lag. However, it was implausible that people would continue to look to the past when they are continuously confronted with higher inflation: they would learn to predict that future inflation would be even higher than the current level. It is clear that inflation expectations are important for the determination of inflation trends. Most prices are set by firms in an administrative fashion, with the expectation that prices will be fixed for a period of time. (However, some prices, such as gasoline, are highly visible and change regularly.) If the man-

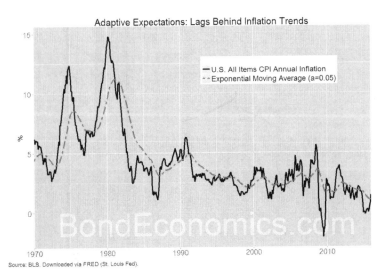

Adaptive Expectations: Lags Behind Inflation Trends

— U.S. All Items CPI Annual Inflation
-- Exponential Moving Average (a=0.05)

Source: BLS. Downloaded via FRED (St. Louis Fed).

agers at the firms expect inflating prices in their input costs, they will raise selling prices to compensate. Therefore, rising inflation expectations raise inflation pretty much by definition.

The problem with the focus on inflation expectations revolves around their use in practice: how do you measure them, and what causes them to move?

Measuring inflation expectations appears straightforward, but the quality of the estimates is often debatable. One possibility is to use surveys, which are typically of economists or consumers. Unfortunately, consumers can be highly sensitive to gasoline prices. As a result, consumer inflation surveys can be infected by spikes in oil prices. However, these events have been misleading, as oil price spikes have not created a wider price spiral in the post-1990 era. Meanwhile, surveys of economists can be influenced by groupthink, and it is unclear how representative their views are. Alternatively, it is possible to infer expected inflation from the pricing of inflation-linked bonds. These bonds are discussed in Section 4.5, but once again, it is unclear whether bond investors' views about inflation represent those of the broader public. (Moreover, the implied inflation expectation can be affected by technical factors within the bond market, as discussed in that section.)

What determines inflation expectations is a more difficult question. Mainstream economics appears to have a simple answer – central bank policy determines inflation expectations. If we verbally interpret the mathematics within the models, the central bank essentially threatens to destroy the economy with ultra-high interest rates unless the inflation rate adheres exactly to its inflation target. As a result, all the central bank needs to do is announce a new target for inflation, and the other entities within the model have no choice but to comply with that dictate.

Within an economic model specified by a handful of equations, such a simplified mechanism is defensible. However, it certainly is not literally true. Central banks currently have a strong hand to fight inflation, but they do not have the political mandate to crush the economy utterly in order to stamp out tiny deviations in the inflation rate from target. In the real world, the reasonable expectation is that inflation will be "near" the target rate, with "near" often translating into a range of about 1% on either side of the inflation target. Furthermore, the expectation is that core inflation (the inflation rate after stripping out energy and food prices) is the inflation rate that will remain near target. That is, "headline" inflation (inflation rates including all components) will deviate from the target by greater amounts.

Unfortunately, the control of inflation is now squishy. Even if we know that inflation is near 2%, this does not tell us whether it will be 1% or 3%. What causes inflation expectations to drift from 1% to 3% (and back again)? It appears that this drift is associated with the state of the economy: when it is stronger, inflation sticks near the top end of the band, and when the economy is weaker, inflation is typically at the bottom end of the band. The measure of the strength of the economy used is typically the output gap – described in the next section.

2.4 The Output Gap and NAIRU

It is clear that expectations alone cannot drive inflation; it is also a function of how the economy is evolving. Over time, we observe that inflation rates move with the cycle. That is,

1. inflation rises during an economic expansion; and
2. it falls during a recession.

Although this observation holds up across countries and over time, the issue is that a great number of other economic variables also rise and fall with the cycle. If we want to model inflation, we can pick any number of these variables, and they would show some correlation with inflation. This means that it is possible to cobble together any number of inflation models, and it is difficult to choose between them. The consensus view at central banks was to gravitate towards the broadest measure of "overheating" of the economy – the output gap. Instead of looking at a few narrowly defined variables, this measure looks at the pace of growth of the entire economy – real Gross Domestic Product (GDP). (*Real Gross Domestic Product* is adjusted for the effect of inflation; *nominal*

Gross Domestic Product is measured in current dollar values.)

Definition The formal definition of the output gap is:

(Output Gap) = (Actual Real GDP) – (Potential Real GDP).

This definition means that if real GDP is above potential GDP, the output gap is positive, whereas it is negative if real GDP is below potential GDP. Note that the output gap is typically specified as a percentage of GDP, so the above measure is then typically divided by real GDP to get the quoted value.

This concept is perfectly sensible from a big picture point of view. The unfortunate problem is that there is no obvious way to measure potential GDP, particularly in "real time." (In economics, a variable can be *estimated in real time* if we can calculate it using currently available data. Otherwise, we have to wait for data to be available to do the calculation, and in some cases, it can take years for the data to arrive. These "non-real time" concepts are useful for economic historians, but are largely useless for economic forecasters.)

The chart below shows a technique to generate a trend GDP value – the Hodrick-Prescott Filter, which is often called the HP Filter. It generates a trend value using a relatively complex algo-

Author calculations. GDP Data Source: BEA. Downloaded via FRED.

rithm. It appeared to offer a standard for estimating series trends.

Unfortunately, the results of the HP filter can be quite misleading. The output of the filter will be revised as new data appear. The chart below shows how the estimated output gap changes as new data are added to the time series. The black line shows the estimated output gap series as it was calculated in 2007 (black line), and then how the series was revised in response to added data (red line). As can be seen, the estimate for the output gap in 2007 switched from a negative value to a large positive value in response to data incorporating the recession that started in December 2007. The possibility of such unreliability makes the filter essentially useless for analysis of the current state of the economy.

Any other techniques to generate a trend GDP value based solely upon actual GDP will face the same problems as the HP filter. This has driven economists at central banks and statistical agencies to move towards other techniques to estimate potential GDP. The standard appears to be using "production function"-based techniques, in which potential output is based on the amount of capital and the size of the labour force. However, since the estimates of the capital stock are not very well developed, the emphasis is upon the slack in the labour market.

As a result, these techniques end up attempting to estimate

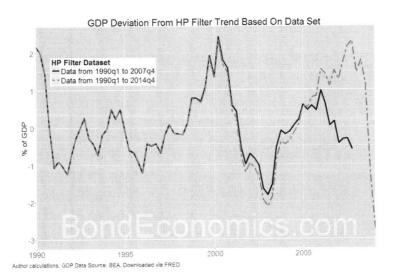

Author calculations. GDP Data Source: BEA. Downloaded via FRED.

what was once called the "natural rate of unemployment," although great lengths are now taken to avoid using that expression in the literature. The term natural rate of unemployment had been replaced by NAIRU – the nonaccelerating inflation rate of unemployment. The term NAIRU has since fallen into disfavour as well, partly as it makes no sense linguistically. This report will use these terms "NAIRU" and "natural rate of unemployment" interchangeably, since these concepts are being presented in a somewhat simplified fashion.

The importance of the labour market in inflation determination has a long history, with one notable early example being the Phillips Curve. From my perspective as an outsider, the differences between various formulations seem small, and it is hard to see how debates over them generated the controversy that they did. For those with an interest in that history, I recommend the text *Full Employment Abandoned: Shifting Sands and Policy Failures*, by William Mitchell and Joan Muysken.

Definition The *natural rate of unemployment* is the rate of unemployment at which the labour market is "balanced," and it provides no upward pressure on inflation.

The usefulness of the natural rate of unemployment is that it allows us to define the *unemployment gap* – which is similar to the output gap (which is why we are interested in the concept in the first place).

Definition The *unemployment gap* is the difference between the current unemployment rate and the "natural" rate (with a positive number indicating that unemployment is greater than the natural rate).

The expectation is that a positive unemployment gap will result in downward pressure on inflation, whereas a negative unemployment gap results in upward pressure on inflation. (This sign convention is the opposite for the output gap.)

Although the "natural rate of unemployment" was first thought of as being a fixed percentage, any attempt at estimating it found that it varied over time (as well as across countries). Therefore, the objective is to come up with an estimate of this "natural rate," which then is mapped to potential GDP. The unemployment gap is effectively a stand-in for the output gap.

The instability of the "natural rate" estimate indicated that it was hardly set by a "law of nature." (The instability of NAIRU was an important part of the debate about monetary policy in the 1990s; it will be discussed further in Section 3.4.) In fact, it depends upon the economic structure. For example, the argument of Modern Monetary Theory (MMT) is that involuntary unemployment could be eliminated by a Job Guarantee scheme, but without creating upward pressure on inflation. However, in the current economic system, people are pushed into involuntary unemployment in order to contain inflation. From the perspective of MMT, the current system keeps citizens unemployed in the same way that "buffer stocks" are used in schemes to manage commodity prices.

We will now return to how this concept is used in the determination of the output gap. The unemployment gap is used as a proxy for the output gap (modulo the flip in sign). Economists previously used the HP filter to estimate unemployment gaps, but that had the defects noted earlier. The core of most modern estimation techniques is a Kalman filter, named after the prominent systems theorist, Rudolf E. Kálmán. The Kalman filter creates and continuously updates an estimate of a state variable, taking into account *assumed* model dynamics.

To give an example of how this works, assume that we have arrived at a highly simplified economic model where the change in the inflation rate over a quarter is equal to 10% of the output gap (as a percentage of GDP). If we observe that the inflation rate is steadily falling at a rate of 0.20% per quarter, we would infer that the output gap is -2% of GDP.

(Please note that I have deliberately simplified matters here, as I am discussing the procedure for a single variable – the output gap. The models used by central banks would simultaneously estimate several variables. The basic principle I describe remains.)

On its face, the estimation procedure seems reasonable. However, we have to be careful about what our model is telling us.

We cannot do things like plot the estimated output gap, and argue that the negative output gap is *causing* inflation to fall. Since the output gap only exists as a result of being inferred from the behaviour of inflation, all we can say is that *changes in the inflation rate cause the estimated output gap to move.*

The result is that all of these statistical techniques create a non-falsifiable closed loop of logic. Since they assume that the output gap drives inflation, but as there is no way of calculating the output gap without reference to how it supposedly causes inflation to move, there is no way of finding data that contradicts the model. The problem is that a theory that is consistent with any observed data ("non-falsifiable") actually tells us very little.

In summary, the output gap concept provides a reasonable framework for thinking about inflation. However, we do not have particularly reliable means of estimating it (or the related unemployment gap) in real time, which is what central banks need to do. Therefore, we need to fall back on watching a wide variety of capacity indicators, which is essentially a more generalised output gap. For example, the Bank of Canada maintains a web page of "Indicators of Capacity and Inflation Pressures for Canada" (URL: http://www.bankofcanada.ca/rates/indicators/capacity-and-inflation-pressures/). Using a mixture of capacity indicators is more subjective, but poses less risk of model dependence.

2.5 Real Rates

Once we assume that the primary objective of central banks is to target the rate of inflation, we then turn to the question of how this is accomplished. The usual response is that the central bank sets the *real* interest rate (the nominal interest rate less the rate of inflation) in such a way that it can control inflation.

The central bank can control inflation in two ways:

1. monetary policy can influence the real growth rate of the economy, which affects inflation via the output gap (Section 2.4);
2. monetary policy can influence inflation expectations, which directly drive inflation, but may have no effect on

real growth.

I am going to treat these two mechanisms as being equivalent, although there are some technical differences. For example, a shift in inflation expectations can have an immediate effect on inflation, whereas the effect of a changing output gap presumably takes time to have an effect on inflation.

Even if we set aside whether the central bank affects the real economy or just expectations, it leaves open the question *How can monetary policy affect inflation expectations or real growth rates?*

One traditional answer is that central banks affect the economy via their alleged control of the money supply. (The simplest version of this theory is the Quantity Theory of Money, which has a long history, but currently is not taken too seriously by most economists.) Post-Keynesian theory rejects the importance of the money supply (although opinions can differ about details). Chapter 4 of Marc Lavoie's *Post-Keynesian Economics* describes this debate, and it is briefly treated in Section 5.4 of my report *Understanding Government Finance*. Since this topic has been heavily discussed elsewhere, this report will not delve too far into that topic. In order to give an empirical reason why the Quantity Theory of Money is dubious, one could study the inability of quantitative easing (the purchase of bonds by the central bank in order to increase the size of the money supply) to raise inflation rates in either Japan or the United States.

Once we give up on the Quantity Theory of Money, we are left with interest rates as the mechanism by which monetary policy influences the economy. I am somewhat skeptical about the sensitivity of the economy to interest rates. As a result, I have reservations about the mechanisms discussed in this section; Section 2.9 discusses these reservations. Nevertheless, even if I am correct, central bankers are strong believers in the effectiveness of interest rates. What matters for bond investors is guessing what central bankers will do, not what I think, so it is important to understand *their* thought processes.

The core belief of conventional economic analysis is that in order to judge the effect of interest rates on the economy, you need to look at the real interest rate, not the nominal interest rate.

Definition The *real interest rate* is the nominal (quoted) interest rate less the rate of inflation (or the expected rate of inflation).

Normally, we look at the short-term real rate, so there should be little difference between the current rate of inflation and the measured rate of inflation (as calculated by looking at the annual rate of change of a price index). The only way a significant gap could open up between those two variables would be in a severely inflationary environment.

When we discuss "real bond yields" we should look at the yield on inflation-linked bonds, and not subtract the rate of inflation from a conventional bond yield. This is because we should not compare the current level of inflation with the expected return over the lifetime of a bond. Inflation-linked bonds are analysed further in Section 4.5.

Why would we adjust interest rates for inflation? The idea is that we want to compare the attractiveness of real goods now versus the future. Assume that you are running a corner store, and that you expect the price of goods to rise by 2% over the next year.

- If you can borrow at 1% interest (which corresponds to a -1% real rate of interest), it is profitable to borrow to buy inventory. For every $100 of inventory you order, it should be worth $102 in a year, but you will only owe $101 on the loan. You have an incentive to order as much inventory as you can finance and store.
- If you can borrow at 5% interest (a 3% real interest rate), it is costly to borrow to buy inventory. In one year, $100 inventory will be worth $102, but you will owe $105 on the loan. You only want to hold the minimum of inventory that you believe that you need to run your business without disruptions.

The key point to note in my description is that this is a *belief* – that real interest rates matter for growth is assumed to hold within mainstream economic models. It is unclear whether real interest rates are practically significant in the current environment. For example, housing finance decisions are highly sensitive to the level of nominal interest rates (as they determine the cost of financing a house), while it is difficult to see how an increase in grocery costs will affect the housing market.

In any event, qualitative statements about "high" or "low" real interest rates is not enough for modern, quantitative approaches in economics. Some form of mathematical statement is needed. This is where the "Natural Rate of Interest" comes in, as discussed in the next section.

2.6 The Natural Rate of Interest

The natural rate of interest is a core concept of mainstream macro, with a long intellectual history. This pedigree has resulted in the concept being widely accepted, even though its usefulness is not entirely clear if you question the hidden assumptions.

It is probably a mistake to assume that the Natural Rate of Interest corresponds to an underlying real world concept; it is far more insubstantial than other non-directly measured concepts used in mainstream economics, like potential GDP or even NAIRU. Those concepts correspond somewhat directly to observed economic series, and one could possibly hope to pin them down via different econometric methods. That is, we should be able to come up with the same estimate of those variables starting from different analytical starting points. Instead, the natural rate of interest is inherently a model-based concept; we cannot infer its value without referring to a model. Furthermore, different models could end up implying different values for the natural rate of interest.

Definition The *natural rate of interest* is the setting of the real policy interest rate that is neutral for the economy, if the economy is growing at potential.

- If the policy rate is above the natural rate, it will have a tendency to depress growth and inflation.
- If the policy rate is below the natural rate, it will cause those variables to accelerate.

Note that the natural rate is defined in terms of the economy being "at potential" (actual GDP matches potential GDP), which is almost never the case. If the economy is not at potential, the effect of the policy rate is dependent upon how the model assumes interest rates relate to the economic variables of interest.

The natural rate of interest is the most problematic of the hidden variables that are used in mainstream economics. We can look at the estimate of the output gap, and we can judge the quality of the estimate by comparing it to other economic data that should correspond to the same concept (such as labour market data or capacity utilisation). There is no reason to believe that the natural rate of interest should be any particular value at any given time, so there is no way of rejecting the estimates turned out by a model.

The paper "Why So Slow? A Gradual Return for Interest Rates," by Vasco Cúrdia, illustrates the problem.

The chart below shows a model estimate of the natural rate of interest for the United States. The estimate was near historical conventional estimates of the real natural rate (above 2%), but then dropped like a rock to below -2.5% starting in 2007. Since nominal rates cannot go below zero and inflation has been low and stable (1%-2%), it was impossible for the actual policy rate to be below the natural rate of interest. Slow growth in the current cycle has been widely blamed upon this limitation upon interest rates, which has led to exploratory moves towards negative interest rates.

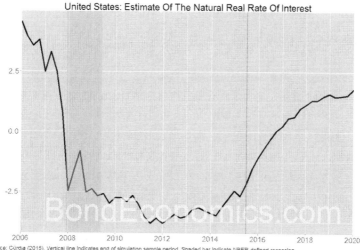

United States: Estimate Of The Natural Real Rate Of Interest

Source: Cúrdia (2015). Vertical line indicates end of simulation sample period. Shaded bar indicate NBER-defined recession.

Beyond 2015q3, the time series is a projection based on the model dynamics. Since whatever has driven the natural rate of interest to be negative is assumed to be temporary, the natural rate reverts to some long-term "normal" level. (The model incorrectly predicted such a reversion throughout the entire negative natural rates period.)

Although it seems that a low natural rate of interest "predicts" the current environment of disappointing growth, in reality it is just the result of the model adjusting state variables to compensate for historical prediction errors. When mainstream models were used in real time at the end of the financial crisis, the estimated value of the natural rate of interest was still positive, and so the consensus expected a rapid recovery. The failure of the methodology was hidden by updating the natural rate estimate so that it was consistent with observed growth. Models that are consistent with any possible outcome tell us very little about the world.

The next section explains how the various analytical building blocks are tied together in order to come up with a suggested policy rate – a Taylor Rule. Although we have reason to be skeptical about these building blocks – such as the natural rate of interest – this deep skepticism is unlikely to be shared by policymakers.

2.7 Taylor Rules

A *Taylor Rule* is a rule that suggests what the level of a central bank's policy rate should be. The original Taylor Rule appeared in the paper "Discretion versus policy rules in practice," by Professor John B. Taylor of Stanford University (which will be referred to here as [Taylor 1993]). A Taylor rule ties the strands of research in the previous sections into a single model that predicts how the central bank should set its policy rate.

Since that first publication, Taylor Rules have been a major area of research for academics, central bankers, and market economists. As a result, there is a wide variety of policy rules generically described as "Taylor Rules."

The chart on the next page gives an updated version of the original [Taylor 1993] rule. There is a key difference, in that I have

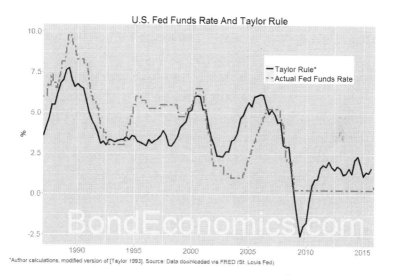

U.S. Fed Funds Rate And Taylor Rule

Taylor Rule*
Actual Fed Funds Rate

*Author calculations, modified version of [Taylor 1993]. Source: Data downloaded via FRED (St. Louis Fed).

used the output gap as calculated by the Congressional Budget Office; whereas [Taylor 1993] used a measure of GDP deviation from trend. The Taylor Rule policy rate follows similar patterns to the actual rate decisions of the Federal Reserve, but the gap between the rule output and the actual rate can be significant.

The formula that generates the Taylor Rule shown in the previous chart is specified by:

$$n(t) = 2\% + p(t) + 0.5\,O(t) + 0.5(p(t)-2\%),$$

where:

- $n(t)$ is the nominal interest rate (Taylor Rule output)
- $p(t)$ is the annual inflation of the GDP deflator
- $O(t)$ is the (CBO) output gap (as a percentage of real GDP)
- the "natural real interest rate" is assumed to be 2% (the first 2% term in the equation)
- and the Fed is implicitly assumed to be targeting a 2% rate of inflation in the GDP deflator (the term $(p(t)-2\%)$ is the deviation of inflation from target)

More generally, the terms in the above equation can be changed by the researcher constructing the rule. For example, the "natural rate of interest" can be allowed to vary over time (as discussed in Section 2.6). Furthermore, there is considerable scope to change the inflation series used.

Three broad strands of research are associated with Taylor rules.

1. Determining a rule that best fits how a central bank reacts to data (widely known as the "reaction function"), and then using this rule to forecast the policy rate. This is extremely common in market research.

2. Dynamic Stochastic General Equilibrium (DSGE) models use the assumption that economic outcomes are the result of optimising decisions of households. Since the optimisation is forward-looking (in the extreme, until time goes to infinity), households need to embed a reaction function for the central bank, as otherwise the future trajectory of interest rates is undefined. Therefore, every DSGE model has to have a reaction function, which is commonly some variant of a Taylor Rule (although more complex dynamics can be used, such as "optimal control" rules). Since central banks are major users of DSGE models, the properties of reaction functions are heavily scrutinised.

3. Is rules-based policy superior to "discretionary" policy? This was the focus of the [Taylor 1993] paper, and Professor Taylor has continued this argument since then. For example, he argues that the housing bubble of the 2000s was the result of too-low policy rates; that is, the fed funds rate was too far below Taylor rule after 2003 (discussed further in Section 3.5.)

In principle, an accurate Taylor Rule would be an extremely valuable tool for a fixed income analyst. All you would need to do is to forecast the components, and you could then then come up with an accurate forecast for the path of the policy rate. This in turn would make bond market investing into a proverbial money-printing machine. Unfortunately, any experience with market research tells you that any halfway-competent economist has a Taylor Rule that validates their view of policy rates – *no matter what that view is*.

A Taylor Rule is an economic Rorschach test, in which economists can project whatever their views are onto the final result. Almost every term within a Taylor Rule is based upon variables that are not measured directly, and these terms are tied together by somewhat arbitrary parameters. The freedom to choose the weighting parameters (within limits) means that there is considerable ability to get the output of the rule near historical policy rates. The researcher can then data mine the possible inputs so that the deviation at the endpoint matches their (or their bosses') preconceived view as to where the policy rate should be right now. The Taylor Rule can then be "improved" when its fit deteriorates or the desired output changes.

In the Appendix (Section A.1), I discuss how I generated the chart below. A very large number of Taylor Rules were developed, which were all deemed to have an "acceptable" relationship to the policy rate. For each date, the maximum and minimum values of any of the rules are plotted. As we can see, the range of interest rates that are suggested by some rule is quite large, and often on both sides of the actual policy rate.

In summary, Taylor Rules are only guidelines. The value of these rules lies in the fact that they tell us what factors a central bank is probably looking at when setting rates. A real world central bank is unlikely to explicitly follow a Taylor Rule, but it seems likely that we will always be able to back-fit some rule to the historical path of the policy rate.

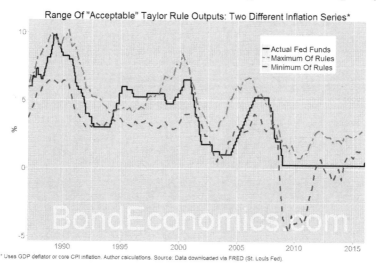

Range Of "Acceptable" Taylor Rule Outputs: Two Different Inflation Series*

— Actual Fed Funds
-- Maximum Of Rules
— Minimum Of Rules

* Uses GDP deflator or core CPI inflation. Author calculations. Source: Data downloaded via FRED (St. Louis Fed).

2.8 The Zero Bound

A topic that once seemed to be a largely theoretical exercise has suddenly developed into a practical problem – the zero lower bound (often abbreviated ZLB) for nominal interest rates. Due to persistent weakness in developed economies after the financial crisis, many developed country central banks cut their policy rates to zero, and even to slightly negative rates. Economists used to argue that negative nominal interest rates were essentially impossible to maintain. If banks paid a negative interest rate on deposits, depositors could withdraw cash, which has an implicit interest rate of 0%. (Please note that this is purely a nominal interest rate phenomenon; if the inflation rate is positive, it is straightforward to achieve negative real rates.)

That particular mechanism did not prevent negative interest rates in practice, since large institutions are not going to withdraw large amounts of cash because of the security risks. Banks have a long history of dealing with bank robbers; pension funds do not have much expertise in that field. Correspondingly, central banks have been able to push policy rates to "mildly negative" levels (-0.50% or so). However, there are other institutional features that allow people to lock in non-negative interest rates, such as the ability to pre-pay taxes. Furthermore, there have been hints of financial institutions creating funds that are backed by currency notes, allowing investors to lock in a 0% interest rate (less the management fees). As a result, interest rates cannot get "too negative" (-3%, say) without requiring some institutional changes within the economy. For example, there has arisen a cottage industry of economists calling for the abolition of cash, so that negative interest rates can stick.

If we modify the "zero lower bound" to be "a lower bound somewhere around zero," we can continue to apply the same analytical implications of the zero lower bound. For bond investors, this is quite important for bond yield evaluation in a "low yield" environment. Previously, "low yields" might have been considered 0%-1%; the experience with negative policy rates causes us to revise that range to be -0.5%-0.5%.

Within DSGE economics, the zero lower bound generated a great deal of excitement. It called into the question the previous New Keynesian consensus on fiscal policy. To simplify, fiscal policy was seen as irrelevant as it was trumped by monetary policy. For example, let us assume that the Treasury wanted to stimulate the economy by cutting tax rates. The New Keynesian rejoinder was that the tax cut would accomplish essentially nothing. The economic effect of the tax cut would be cancelled by the central bank in its pursuit of inflation stability. If the economy grew faster, expected inflation would rise above target, and so the central bank would be forced to raise interest rates, cancelling out the stimulus. (The possibility that fiscal policy is used to hit economic targets, while keeping interest rates unchanged, is ignored.) However, the zero lower bound messes up that story. If the policy rate is stuck at its lower bound, it is possible for the DSGE model economy to be stuck with a negative output gap, and inflation expectations to be also stuck below the central bank's target. In this case, the Treasury is free to ramp up spending to stimulate the economy without the central bank cancelling that stimulus.

Even if one agrees with the DSGE modelling methodology, this topic is more complex than it appears. Many of the discussions of the zero lower bound are oversimplified in their treatment of time. Within a full DSGE model, it is not enough that the policy rate is zero right now; it also has to be expected to be zero for an indefinite period. This condition was not actually met in the United States in the post-2009 period, or even in Japan for most of the post-1995 period. Bond yields were positive, and appeared to incorporate an expectation of the policy rate rising above zero within a few years.

The theoretical importance of the zero lower bound (or "almost zero" lower bound) depends upon your view of DSGE economics. Since I am skeptical about DSGE models, I believe this is an unimportant topic. However, central bank staffers are still largely wedded to DSGE economics, and they would not agree with my assessment.

2.9 Conventional Versus Post-Keynesian Approaches

Most of the analysis within this report describes the concepts used by mainstream economics. However, I prefer an alternative tradition for economic theory – post-Keynesian economics. Unfortunately, a full discussion of the differences between post-Keynesian and mainstream economics is well outside the scope of this report. Nevertheless, a focus on mainstream methodology is needed when studying how interest rates are set. The policy rate is administered by a committee of policymakers, who are almost entirely drawn from the mainstream economic tradition. In order to forecast those decisions, we need to understand the methodology behind them. Post-Keynesian economics could only help analysts predict whether policy errors are going to be committed. Unfortunately, policy errors are not easy to diagnose in real time, and that is a topic that has to be deferred to later reports.

Within the context of interest rate determination, there are a few areas of key disagreement between the mainstream and post-Keynesians:

- the relative importance of fiscal and monetary policy
- the importance of interest rates in determining economic activity
- and the inherent stability of a capitalist economy

As discussed in the previous section, the mainstream consensus was that fiscal policy was largely irrelevant. (Although the policy rate hitting 0% called that view into question.) The central bank smoothed the economic cycle; the role of the rest of the government was just to remove structural rigidities so that productivity would increase. Conversely, post-Keynesians stress the importance of fiscal policy. The differences can lead to serious disagreements over policy: the disastrous austerity policies pursued after the financial crisis being an important example. Although this is an important area of debate, it will have to be discussed outside the context of this report.

Post-Keynesian approaches to economics do not start with the assumption that economic activity reflects the optimising choices of households; the mainstream essentially blocks from publication any theoretical paper that does not start from that assumption. Since interest rates are a mechanism to tie together consumption decisions across time, mainstream models embed a strong dependence upon interest rates. Conversely, since post-Keynesian economics has a different starting point, interest rates are of lesser importance.

Moreover, by no longer just assuming the effect of interest rates upon the economy, post-Keynesian economists are more open to the view that the effect of monetary policy is more ambiguous, and can even have the opposite effect than that assumed by mainstream approaches. However, "post-Keynesian economics" is an extremely broad tent, and not all post-Keynesians are skeptical about the role of interest rates in steering the economy. Modern Monetary Theory is the school of thought within post-Keynesian economics with the greatest skepticism about the mainstream story regarding interest rates.

There are a number of reasons why a low interest rate may not cause economic growth to accelerate, or inflation to rise. (The logic can be extended to why high interest rates might not lower inflation.)

- Lower interest rates will lower interest income. This reduces government deficits, and it redistributes income within the private sector. For example, businesses are generally net payers of interest. Increased interest rates would transfer income from businesses to households that live off a fixed income.
- There is little evidence that interest rates have an effect on consumption patterns or investment activity. Businesses invest when faced with high utilisation of their fixed assets.
- Interest rates are a cost of doing business. Lowering interest costs allows businesses to lower prices.
- Interest rates are important for the housing market, but this effect is smaller after a housing bubble pops.

A view that suggests that interest rates have the opposite effect on the economy than what is believed by central bankers is simultaneously extremely entertaining and frightening. It is a possibility that should be kept in mind. However, it is difficult to describe mainstream debates about interest rate policy if the actual effect is the opposite of what is conventionally assumed, and so this non-standard theory will not be discussed further here.

Central bankers are unlikely to embrace a theory that interest rates do not matter very much, as that would greatly lower their status. Therefore, central bank watchers will have to assume that rates are set based upon the presupposition that the level of real interest rates is critical to the functioning of the economy, even if this not the case. The analysis within this report assumes that the mainstream view is directionally correct, but that the effectiveness of interest rates is less than suggested by mainstream analysis.

Finally, mainstream economics models are built around various notions of equilibrium. The dynamics of private sector activity tend to be quite stable, and the only way to generate a business cycle is for there to be some form of "random" disturbance that pushes the economic trajectory away from a steady state. Alternatively, post-Keynesian approaches emphasise the inherent instability of the private sector in a capitalist economy. For those readers who are interested, Marc Lavoie's textbook *Post Keynesian Economics: New Foundations* gives an overview of post-Keynesian economics, aimed at honours undergraduate economics students or Master's students.

The following chapter gives an overview of recent interest rate (and economic) cycles. The fact that each cycle in the United States was associated with some form of financial crisis lends support to the post-Keynesian view that capitalist economies are inherently unstable.

Chapter 3 Modern Interest Rate and Economic Cycles

3.1 Introduction

In the interest of saving space, this report discusses what I call "modern" business cycles, which are those that start after 1990. This is a somewhat boring sample period for fixed income alarmists, as inflation has done almost nothing during this time. The real excitement on the inflation front (with corresponding carnage in the bond markets) happened during the 1970s. I prefer to stick with the post-1990 period, as there appears to be large structural differences in economic performance before and after 1990. If you try to fit a model for the economy or fixed income markets, it is extremely rare that it will work before and after that date. (Equity market behaviour appears to be somewhat more consistent over time.)

There are good reasons for the different economic behaviour in the different eras. These include:

- changes in the operating procedures of central banks
- elimination of wage and price controls as a policy option
- a shrinkage of the public sector
- dismantlement of trade barriers
- a decrease in unionisation
- a decrease in indexation of contracts to inflation
- technological changes allowing for things like "just-in-time" inventory management
- deregulation of interest rate markets

- increased experience with floating rate currencies (the United States only broke the link between the dollar and gold in 1973)
- abandonment of full employment as a policy goal, and changes to the philosophy of labour market regulation

(For the final point, a good reference is the previously cited textbook *Full Employment Abandoned* by William Mitchell and Joan Muysken.)

Given the rather impressive list of differences outlined above, I believe that it is very difficult to compare the present situation to the situation in the 1970s. A similar future rise in inflation is presumably possible, but my feeling is that we would need some of the above-listed structural factors to return to a semblance of the 1970s situation.

If we go further back into post-World War II history, we cannot learn many useful things about interest rate behaviour. Interest rates were regulated, and so interest rate cycles were not particularly significant. The details varied by country, but I am not familiar with any bond market that was not highly regulated during the 1950s and 1960s. (The Japanese Government did not issue long-dated debt, so a yen government bond market did not even exist.) There was some excitement in the financial system, but it mainly revolved around the currency peg system that was in place.

The treatment here will focus heavily on the experience of the United States, with discussions of other developed economies mainly focusing on how they differed from the trajectory of the United States. The differences were fairly pronounced up until the late 1990s, after which we have had an increasingly synchronised global capital market.

3.2 The United States After the S&L Crisis

The United States fell into recession from July 1990 to March 1991 (based on the Business Cycle Dating Committee of the National Bureau Economic Research - NBER). There were a number of factors that led to the recession, including a real estate bubble that was associated with the Savings and Loan banks ("S&L's"), a slowdown in the defence industry as a result of a short-lived "peace dividend" after the end of the Cold War, and a spike in oil prices (coinciding with the invasion of Kuwait). The relevance of the oil price spike with respect to the timing of the recession is discussed further in Section 5.4.

The real estate market – both residential and commercial – was a major contributor to the 1990 recession (although it was smaller than the real estate bubble that led to the Financial Crisis of 2008; chart below). There had been a rather epic amount of speculative investment financed by the recently deregulated S&L's. Professor Bill Black, who was a regulator during the S&L crisis, wrote an excellent history of the period – *The Best Way to Rob A Bank is to Own One.*

The factors that pushed the economy into recession were not particularly unusual when compared to earlier post-war recessions, other than the fact that the financial system was a major factor in destabilising the economy. The financial sector had not caused problems in the early post-war period. Tight regulation, liquid balance sheets, and strong memories of the Great Depression (and the financial sector's role in creating that depression) kept the financial sector in check. However,

U.S. Private Housing Starts*

* Seasonally adjusted, annual rate. Source: Bureau of the Census, downloaded via FRED (St. Louis Fed).

recurrent financial crises started to arise in the 1960s when those stabilising factors started to fade. For many observers, the 1990-1991 recession appeared to be a culmination of the destabilising trends in finance. (This tendency towards destabilisation was a key theme of the work of the economist Hyman Minsky, and is covered in his book *Stabilizing an Unstable Economy*.) Of course, the excesses that led to the Financial Crisis of 2008 make the S&L Crisis look tame in comparison.

The subsequent recovery from the recession of 1990-1991 was seen as unusually slow. Previously, the typical pattern was for economic growth to recover rapidly. The disarray in the housing market, and the tightness of fiscal policy, presumably led to this slow recovery. In retrospect, this slow recovery set the pattern for later recoveries – which economists have now labelled "secular stagnation."

The Fed Funds rate was held at what was seen as an "emergency level" of 3% for 16 months. However, growth eventually returned. Unfortunately for the bond market, this was not foreseen by investors, and so the decision by the Federal Reserve to return the policy rate to "normal levels" came as a costly shock.

One thing that sets the 1994 cycle apart from the following cycles (which I will discuss in later sections) is that the Federal Reserve raised rates in an irregular fashion. Some meetings saw rate hikes of 50 or even 75 basis points, while the policy rate was unchanged at others. (A *basis point* is 0.01%, e.g., 25 basis points = 0.25%.) By contrast, the later cycles saw steady rate hikes of 25 basis points per meeting, a policy mode that is known as "gradualism." I discuss the debate about gradualism in Section 3.5.

In any event, the 1994 rate hike cycle caused considerable losses for fixed income investors. This period was the early days of fixed income derivative trading, and apparently a great many investors had "sold volatility" as a way of enhancing what they viewed as "too low" yields. (Those investors essentially sold insurance against the possibility of increasing interest rates.) Most investors could not properly calculate the risk on their positions, and they managed to blow up quite nicely. If you work in finance and express bullish sentiment about government bonds, expect to hear a great many stories about the 1994 bond bear market.

A crisis in the financial markets finished the 1994 rate hike cycle, which is a common theme of all the interest rate cycles I discuss here. Rising interest rates damaged the perceived creditworthiness of the Mexican government, and the so-called "Tequila Crisis" erupted.

3.3 Other Countries in the Early 1990s

The early-to-mid 1990s was one of the last periods of desynchronised growth amongst the developed countries; trade barriers were still in the process of being dismantled, and the capital markets were still fragmented on a national basis. Since then, developed countries have converged towards a global economic cycle. There were exceptions – Japan was stuck in a low growth path, and economic growth in the euro area has been strangled due to policymaker incompetence.

In this section, I will discuss some of the characteristic features of the Canadian, Japanese, and British cycles during that period. Continental European countries were preparing for entry into the euro, which created a distinctive "convergence" pattern for interest rates. This pattern of behaviour was associated with a fixed exchange rate system, which is outside the scope of this report.

Canada The Canadian economic experience was somewhat similar to that of the United States over this period. There had been local housing and condominium bubbles in the early 1990s (mainly in Toronto and Vancouver), but these caused fewer difficulties than the S&L crisis in the United States.

The Canadian economy had a larger amount of government intervention than the United States, and there was persistent high inflation throughout the 1980s. This was politically unpopular, and Canada moved to an inflation-targeting regime that took effect in 1992 (it was announced in 1991). The early 1990s recession was severe, and knocked out the momentum behind inflation. Inflation has since been quite close to the Bank of Canada's target of 2%, with deviations usually the result of oil price swings (next page).

Canada CPI Inflation And Target Range

Blue box indicates target range of 1-3%. Source: Statistics Canada via CANSIM.

The Canadian Federal Government tightened fiscal policy, cutting back on spending. This eventually led to fiscal surpluses. This experience has led many Canadians to believe that fiscal surpluses are a normal state of affairs, while they are actually an unusual outcome. (The use of stock-flow consistent models – known as SFC models – explains why this is true. If nominal incomes are growing in the private sector, the expectation is that investors will want to hold increasing amounts of government debt. This debt can only be created if the government runs persistent fiscal deficits.) This tight fiscal policy helped dampen economic growth; the Canadian economy consistently under-performed the American over this period (and the American economy itself was sluggish by its historical standards).

Monetary conditions needed to be loose to counteract the tightness of fiscal policy. Interest rates were relatively low, and the Canadian dollar weakened considerably. (This relationship between interest rates and the currency is discussed further in Section 4.6.)

Japan The Japanese economy and bond market moved to its own rhythm during the period discussed in this report. Japan had been riding an economic growth wave since the end of World War II. The Japanese built an export machine, and the proceeds of their surpluses led to high-profile foreign acquisitions. Unfor-

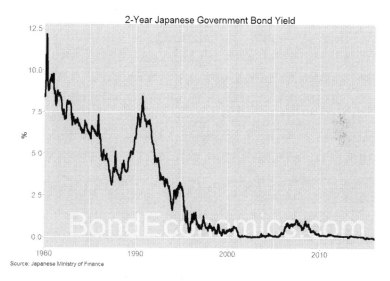

2-Year Japanese Government Bond Yield

Source: Japanese Ministry of Finance

tunately, strong growth led to exuberant behaviour, and an epic stock market and land price bubble. Since land was often used as collateral for loans (the Japanese industrial system was built around bank lending, much like European countries), rising land prices allowed borrowers to leverage up their balance sheets. The burst of the twin bubbles led to a long period of sluggish growth. The policy rate dropped to zero, and largely stayed there for decades (chart above). Although we are now becoming accustomed to low nominal interest rates, Japanese in-

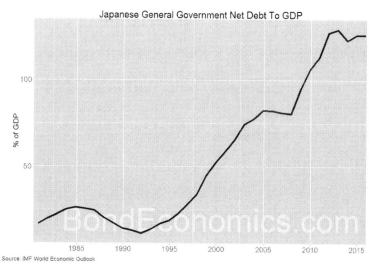

Japanese General Government Net Debt To GDP

Source: IMF World Economic Outlook

terest rates were a novelty in the mid-1990s. What was especially troubling for conventional analysts was that these low interest rates coincided with high levels of government debt. Interest rate analysts have been entertained by a circus parade of "experts" pronouncing that Japanese bond yields are "unsustainable," and that the Japanese Government Bond (JGB) market would melt down within months. The JGB market pricing was more "sustainable" than the "experts'" short positions.

The policy stasis in Japan was unusual; there were essentially no interest rate cycles over the period in question. Instead, the focus of policy makers was on the currency. Japan is one of the few developed countries that intervened in the currency markets in order to support exports in the post-1990 era. (Switzerland attempted to maintain a currency peg in 2014-2015, which blew up in the face of its central bank.) During the 1980s, developed countries were more likely to intervene in currency markets, as floating currencies were still a novelty. However, the consensus in most countries (outside of Japan) moved to the view that currency interventions accomplished little. Although there has been a great deal of public worrying about deflation in Japan *(deflation is a negative inflation rate, i.e., falling prices)*, the better characterisation is that Japan has achieved

Japan Level of Consumer Price Index (CPI)*

* CPI all items ex-imputed rent. Source: e-Stat (Japan).

price level stability. As shown in the chart on the previous page, the level of the CPI index (excluding imputed rent) has stuck within a range that is 5% wide since 1992 (the 100-105 levels on the chart). Although supporters of the Gold Standard trumpet the stability of the price level it achieved, the Japanese experience may represent an even greater stabilisation of the price level.

The United Kingdom Our small survey of countries concludes with the U.K. experience. The chart below shows the path of the discount rate in the United Kingdom. The very high rates around 1990 stand out, and are the result of currency peg economics.

At that time, the United Kingdom was a member of the Exchange Rate Mechanism (ERM), which was a European fixed exchange rate system that was the forerunner of the euro. During the late 1980s, the U.K. government set interest rates at a low level, which helped fuel speculation in the housing market ("the Lawson Boom"). Unfortunately, geopolitics rained on the parade of those mortgage borrowers. When East Germany was reunited with West Germany, the Bundesbank (the German central bank, which has been the *de facto* central bank for continental Europe for decades) hiked interest rates in order to dampen the inflationary impact of the reunification. The Bank of England had no choice but to fol-

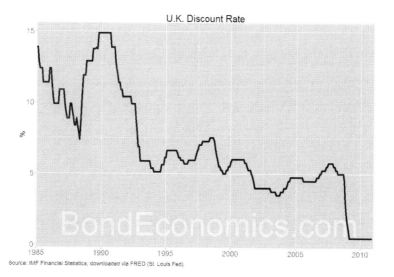

U.K. Discount Rate

Source: IMF Financial Statistics, downloaded via FRED (St. Louis Fed)

low the Bundesbank's lead, which crushed the property market.

The economic pressure became unbearable, and speculation arose that the U.K. would be forced out of the ERM. When hiking interest rates twice in a day failed to reduce the pressure on the pound, the U.K. government threw in the towel and let the currency float.

Hiking interest rates to defend currencies like that is a common policy action in a currency peg regime; they are largely absent once the authorities embrace the freedom provided by a floating currency. This is seen in the examples I provide here, where interest rates were largely set based on conditions in the domestic economy.

Once the U.K. left the ERM, the Bank of England was free to focus on the domestic economy. Inflation stabilised, and the policy rate was relatively stable – much less volatile than the U.K. in the 1980s, and somewhat less volatile than the United States over that period. Mortgages in the U.K. tend to be floating, and thus the household sector was sensitive to movements in the policy rate.

By 1997 or so, the economic cycles of the developed economies (possibly excluding Japan) acted in a more synchronised fashion. We turn next to the U.S. economic experience in the late 1990s.

3.4 Telecom Boom

The aftermath of the Tequila Crisis (and other financial market disturbances) led to the Federal Reserve walking back

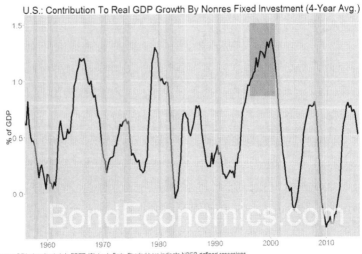

U.S.: Contribution To Real GDP Growth By Nonres Fixed Investment (4-Year Avg.)

Source: BEA. downloaded via FRED (St. Louis Fed). Shaded bars indicate NBER-defined recessions.

some of the previous rate hikes in 1995-6. The following period exhibited relative stability in the policy rate, with only a
small rate cycle around the 1998 LTCM crisis. However, that
stability ended in 2001, when the Fed once again resorted to
drastic rate cuts. The effects of a technology boom dominated this period, which is one of the last "classic" business cycles generated by a boom in non-residential fixed investment.

The previous chart shows the average contribution to growth
over 4-year windows by non-residential fixed investment. (For
example, the value shown for the first quarter of the year 2000
represents the average contribution to growth over the four
years ending at that quarter.) This average hit a maximum of
1.37% in April 2000, which was a post-war maximum (the period of interest is highlighted). Although the short-term impact
of investment hit higher peaks during earlier eras, the 1990s
investment boom stands out for the length of time it was sustained. It should be noted that the chart above references all
non-residential investment, and not just the technology category.
Therefore, even though we associate the exuberance of the period with technology firms, it was the last period when corporate managers were willing to undertake hefty fixed investment.

The investment boom was entwined with a boom in the eq-

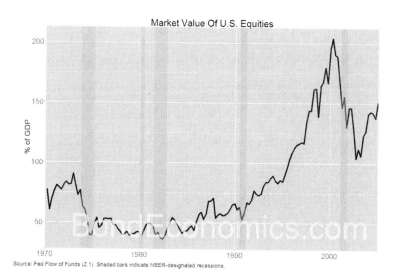

Market Value Of U.S. Equities

Source: Fed Flow of Funds (Z.1). Shaded bars indicate NBER-designated recessions.

uity market. As the previous chart shows, the ratio of the market value of equities to GDP had dropped during the high inflation 1970s, and meandered around 50% until the early 1990s. The period of stable inflation was a boon to equity valuation, and the market value marched steadily higher. The spectacle of rising wealth fueled the "animal spirits" of capitalism, which presumably helped boost investment. As discussed in Section 5.3, the action of the Kalecki Profit Equation meant that higher investment led to higher profits, validating the views of equity market bulls.

The behaviour of the labour market challenged the Fed's understanding of the economy during this period. The unemployment rate steadily marched lower, right through the level of NAIRU (Section 2.4; chart below). Hawkish central bankers called for rate hikes, as they believed the labour market was on the verge of overheating, and rekindling inflation. However, Fed Chairman Alan Greenspan did not hike rates in reaction to that development, instead arguing that rising productivity (related to the technology boom) would keep inflation under control. The lack of inflation validated Greenspan's view, and was probably the episode which most contributed to his positive reputation as a central banker. (Greenspan's critics generally point to his alleged role in the creation of the housing bubble as a negative legacy.)

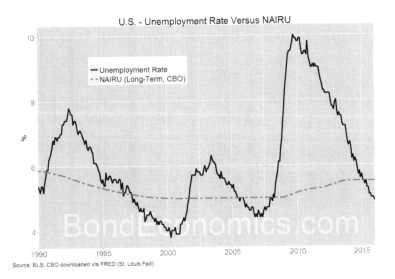

Comments here just provide an overview of what was an extensive debate. Since we now have access to decades of additional economic data, the concern is not what happened then, rather how the developments were perceived in real time. I would suggest two brief summaries for those who are interested in further background.

- The paper "What Have We Learned since October 1979?", by Alan S. Blinder, gives a short summary of that era.
- The Ball and Mankiw paper "The NAIRU in Theory and Practice" is sympathetic to NAIRU, and discusses the various theories advanced to explain why NAIRU was apparently lower than expected.

The bottom line from this episode is that we need to be somewhat skeptical about the various non-measured variables like NAIRU that drive modern economic models. Even if we are sympathetic to the concept underlying the non-measured variable, we need to crosscheck against observed economic series.

Another factor that stretched out the cycle in the United States was globalisation. A number of Asian economies ("the Asian Tigers") followed the example of Japan and its export-led strategies. Manufacturing capacity was built up, and goods markets were increasingly over-supplied. Furthermore, many private firms

U.S. Import Price Index: Consumer Goods, Ex-Automobiles

Persistent price falls
during the late 1990s

Source: BLS, downloaded via FRED (St. Louis Fed). Shaded bars indicate NBER-defined recessions.

borrowed in U.S. dollars, as their home currencies were largely pegged against the U.S. dollar. However, this borrowing proved to be unsustainable. The Asian economies went into a tailspin ("the Asian Crisis"), accentuated by disastrous austerity policies recommended by the International Monetary Fund. As seen in the chart on the previous page, the second half of the 1990s saw an outright fall in the price index for U.S. consumer goods imports (the series in the chart excludes autos). This "imported deflation" also kept price pressures under control, which also allowed the Federal Reserve to remain mainly on the sidelines. It is arguable that this may have helped stretch out the 1990s expansion in the United States. (The situation was far worse for the Asian economies, of course.)

Eventually, the excesses in technology investment were so large that it became apparent that there was massive overcapacity in the telecom sector. Furthermore, the European telecom firms bid up the prices of 3G wireless licences, and wrecked their credit ratings. The national telecoms' operators started out AAA-rated in the mid-1990s, and most ended up clinging to the bottom rung of the investment grade (BBB-rated) by the end of the boom. Once the credit taps were turned off for these firms, capital expenditures were slashed as the firms switched modes from reckless expansion to survival. The collapse in capital expenditures hit the telecom equipment makers, which had previously been stock market darlings.

At the same time, the equity market had become completely unhinged from economic reality, and speculators were bidding up anything with "dot-com" in their name. (In Canada, observers were entertained by dubious shell companies that were allegedly engaging in mining exploration suddenly announcing Internet strategies and seeing their stock prices jump.) Although the breakdown in common sense by equity investors was impressive, the excesses in the initial public offering (IPO) market were still a sideshow. Those IPOs were a mechanism to transfer wealth from speculators to insiders (and bankers), but it was just a zero-sum transfer of money (much like casino or sports betting). Capital expenditures by large firms drove growth, and those expenditures went into reverse when the credit markets tightened lending terms. (To their credit, developed country banking systems managed to avoid blowing themselves up with bad loans during the technology bubble. Unfortunately, this meant that the banks believed their own propaganda about their risk management expertise, and they walked into an even bigger trap in the following decade.)

In summary, the 1990s saw a long-lived expansion in the United States (and many other developed countries). A crisis in the financial markets ended the expansion when the end of the flow of credit undercut fixed investment.

3.5 The 2000s Expansion and the Financial Crisis

The expansion that took place in the early- to mid-2000s was global in scope, and was cut off by the Financial Crisis, which was the most wrenching economic event in the developed world since the Great Depression. The comments in this section will be extremely brief, as the Financial Crisis and it origins has been a topic of considerable debate elsewhere.

The difficulty in discussing the Financial Crisis is that it was caused by a mixture of complex and simple elements. Therefore, it is easy to either come up with a simple explanation for the episode, or else one can end up being buried in complex details.

My view is that the Financial Crisis can be explained relatively easily, but the driving force behind it is not normally thought about. It was the result of the trends on portfolio investors' balance sheets. Decades of deregulation, as well as the growth of those balance sheets versus national income, meant that portfolio flows have become key determinants of developments in the real economy. For example, pension policies in the developed world have had the result that increasing amounts of assets have built up in funds whose sole objective is to keep growing. Mainstream models did not incorporate these balance sheet effects, and so these trends were ignored by policymakers. (Since the crisis, various attempts have been made to incorporate them into models, with debatable success.) The economist Hyman Minsky is most associated with discussing those balance sheet effects (and he stated that he was just following the lead of Keynes); I quickly summarise how this view of the business cycle differs from the mainstream in Section 5.3.

The complexity of the Financial Crisis revolves around how the portfolio affected the real economy. All of the major investors involved were global in scope, and so the breakdown of the economy followed the pattern of the breakdown in the wholesale funding markets. Those funding markets are opaque, and even the regulators had a hard time understanding what was happening until it was too late. Since those developments in funding markets did not affect how central banks set interest rates (at least until the crisis hit), this report will focus on the debate about interest rates.

After the crisis, there have been two (somewhat related) complaints regarding how the Federal Reserve set interest rates before 2007.

1. The Federal Reserve kept interest rates "too low" before the crisis (for example, relative to a Taylor Rule), which led to destabilising speculative activity.

2. When the Federal Reserve raised rates, it did it in too predictable a manner (25 basis points at every scheduled meeting).

The argument that the Federal Reserve set interest rates too low is interesting, but it raises awkward questions for mainstream

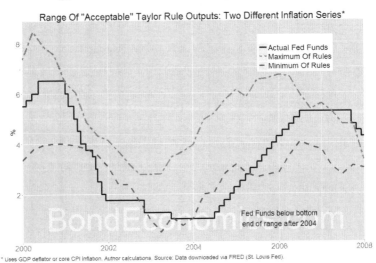

Range Of "Acceptable" Taylor Rule Outputs: Two Different Inflation Series*

* Uses GDP deflator or core CPI inflation. Author calculations. Source: Data downloaded via FRED (St. Louis Fed).

theory. The previous chart illustrates the core of the argument. It compares the actual Fed Funds rate to the range of Taylor Rule outputs – as discussed in Section 2.7 – during the 2000s. The actual rate was below the lower end of the range. Analysts generally put forth a preferred rule, and they will often see the same result (actual policy rate lower than the rule).

The problem with this argument is that the inflation rate was well behaved during the period, as shown in the chart below. The Federal Reserve was essentially acting as an inflation-targeting central bank – which is what most mainstream economists were calling for during the period. *From the standpoint of inflation targeting, the central bank's decisions were not mistaken.* Complaining that "too low" interest rates "caused" speculation and the Financial Crisis is moving the goalposts after the game is over. One can argue that this episode shows that a sole focus on inflation targeting was a bad idea (which is exactly what many post-Keynesians were saying before the crisis), but that does not mean that the central bank failed in what it was trying to do. Even if we replace inflation targeting with a more sensible objective ("macroprudential supervision" being a current piece of jargon), the central bank is just as likely to fail in meeting that new objective. Any policy framework that relies on an omniscient central plan-

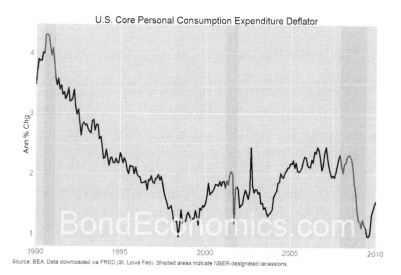

U.S. Core Personal Consumption Expenditure Deflator

Source: BEA. Data downloaded via FRED (St. Louis Fed). Shaded areas indicate NBER-designated recessions.

ning committee administering policy rates is going to run into the same problems that faced the Federal Reserve in the 2000s.

The counterfactual scenario (the Federal Reserve raises rates more rapidly, in line with various Taylor Rules) has some difficulties.

- If you believe that the real economy is highly sensitive to interest rates (as suggested by mainstream models), then the "correct" path for interest rates would have had to be within 100-200 basis points of the historical policy rate. If not, inflation would have undershot target by assumption.

- If we assume that the real economy is not that sensitive to interest rates, we could imagine that it would have been possible to raise interest rates markedly without causing inflation to undershoot the target. However, under this assumption, it is very hard to argue that a relatively small deviation from a Taylor Rule suggestion makes any difference.

- The level of Treasury yields was far below investors' return targets. A belief that a marginal increase in Treasury yields would have damped speculation seems implausible. Given the tendency of the yield curve to flatten during a rate hike cycle (Section 4.3), the policy rate would have to have risen by far more than is suggested by Taylor Rules in order to have made leveraged speculation unattractive.

This debate is interesting, but it is now the domain of historians and memoir-writing central bankers. From a forward-looking perspective, it underlines the skepticism we need to have about models in which "benevolent" central bankers steer an economy towards "optimal outcomes." Instead, we need to take into account the wider range of policy options – including fiscal policy – and we need to accept the fact that the central bank faces much more awkward choices than are suggested by models based on a few non-measured variables.

Finally, many commentators have argued that the policy of a steady sequence of 25 basis point rate hikes was a policy error.

This policy is often referred to as "gradualism," as it was branded in a 2004 speech by Ben Bernanke (at the time, he was a governor at the Federal Reserve, and not yet the chairman of the Federal Open Markets Committee). Allegedly, this predictability led market participants to engage in riskier behaviour. Making the rate hikes unpredictable would supposedly inject some volatility into the market, and force investors to be more careful. For example, the meetings during the 1994 cycle featured a mixture of no change, or 25, 50, and even 75 basis point hikes.

Presumably, having the central bank introduce some "random noise" into the policy rate would have the effect of raising term risk premia. That is, it would accentuate a bond bear market (as was the case in 1994). That said, needlessly pushing up term interest rates appears to be a policy error. (In fact, any number of policies are justified on the basis that they will reduce term premia.) Raising the risk premia for term borrowing is economically inefficient; society has to provide an extra reward to lenders in order to compensate for instability being induced by the central bank.

Unless the Federal Reserve greatly increases the number of policy meetings, or else they re-introduce changing the policy rate by one-eighth of a percent (12.5 basis points), there is not a great deal of room for them to mix things up. A pace of 25 basis points per meeting implies a rise in short rates of 200 basis points a year (since there are eight regular monetary policy meetings in a year), which is certainly a fast enough pace to keep up with a Taylor Rule output in the modern era. The inflation rate has been stuck in a range of a couple hundred basis points for a few decades; there has been no need to raise the policy rate by 4% in a year.

Furthermore, none of this really matters for the rates market. Even if we know "for sure" that the Federal Reserve is going to raise the policy rate by 25 basis points per meeting over the next four meetings, this provides negligible insight for pricing most bonds. The only information that is provided is how to price the first coupon on a 10-year bond; we still have to worry about pricing the remaining 19 coupons (and principal).

The only markets where knowledge of the exact path of rate

hikes would matter are for short-dated options on risk-free instruments (Fed Funds, Overnight Indexed Swaps, Treasury bills). Those option markets were extremely small when compared to the options on long-dated instruments. Although many interest rate trade structures blew up during the crisis, I am unaware of any that were associated with the behaviour of the Federal Reserve. The failures were associated with funding and "balance sheet" trades, almost all of which were hedged against nominal interest rates. (Everybody knew that interest rates were rising, and so the analytical effort was expended upon finding duration neutral positions with good carry.)

We need to look further afield to find the markets where the rate hike pattern allegedly mattered. At which point, we need to ask, why would those markets be priced based on the sequence of Fed rate hikes? The most notable example I have seen raised is the alleged effect of the Federal Reserve on equity (and credit) investors.

Although some equity strategists may have been blaming equity market moves upon central bank decisions, this probably is just an attempt to come up with an after-the-fact explanation for market movements that would have happened anyway. If you want to buy shares in a company, you should be valuing them based on the expected dividends that will be received far into the dim future – and not what the level of the overnight rate will be over the next six weeks. Unfortunately, a certain amount of lunacy has become standard operating procedure for equity market analysis. Is it reasonable to expect the central bank to act in a random and opaque fashion, just to confuse credulous equity investors?

Finally, there were unsafe financing schemes put into place across the developed world, and not just in the United States. Although the Federal Reserve is important within the global system, interest rates in different currencies do not move in lock step. Gradualism in U.S. rate hikes alone should not be enough to create this global speculation; deeper forces were at work.

In summary, the expansion of the 2000s poses a challenge to the view that the primary role of the central bank is to adjust real interest rates in response to movements in the output gap.

However, it may be that financial market participants will have learned some lessons, so they may act in a less destabilising manner. Meanwhile, central banks presumably have picked up a certain amount of expertise in crisis management. Therefore, we can hope that we can avoid similar crises, and the interest rate cycle may return to following the developments in the real economy.

Chapter 4 Market Reaction to Policy Rate Changes

4.1 Introduction

Central banks set short-term rates, but longer maturity interest rates are generally determined in the market. This is not always the case, as the yields on bonds were set by regulation and the central bank during and after World War II. However, the developed economies generally deregulated bond yields by the 1980s.

Nevertheless, central bank policy is important for the determination of bond yields, despite the appearance that they are set in markets. This is because the fair value for a government bond is determined by the expected path of short rate. This is known as the "rate expectations" view of interest rate formation. This is the consensus method for valuing bonds within finance, although it leaves open the question of term risk premia. This is discussed further in Section 4.2.

When we look at historical data, we see that bond yields follow particular patterns during an interest rate cycle. One important example is how the slope of the yield curve behaves. Slopes are important, as they are used as economic indicators, while dedicated bond investors take relative value positions that are a bet on how the slope will move. In practice, many dedicated bond investors prefer to take positions on the slope of the curve rather than on the direction of interest rates, as the risk is more easily controlled.

4.2 Rate Expectations and Term Premia

Glancing at charts of bond yields and short-term rates shows an obvious relationship between the two. This is not accidental; according to rate expectations theory, the expected path of short-term rates largely determines bond yields. The driver of this relationship is the use of leverage by fixed income investors: the yield of a bond is driven by the cost of financing a levered position in that bond. Complexity increases if we wish to add in the notion of term premia. Long-term bonds have greater price risk, and so should have a higher expected return than short-term instruments. Modern academic techniques probably pay too much attention to term premia; the best way forward as an analyst is to assume that term premia are small and stable.

This report will only provide a non-mathematical overview of this topic. There are longer descriptions available elsewhere, including at BondEconomics.com, and in Appendix A.3 of the report *Understanding Government Finance.*

The rate expectations model makes the following prediction (if the term premium is zero): the yield on a (credit risk free) bond should equal the expected cost of financing the bond at a short-term rate over the bond's lifetime. For government bonds, that financing rate is normally close to the policy rate set by the central bank, and so I will use the shortcut of treating the average financing cost to be equal to the average of the policy rate over a period.

A bond has a *term premium* if its yield is higher than the expected average of short-term rates over the lifetime of the bond. For example, if the policy rate is expected to average 2% over the next two years, and the term premium is 100 basis points (1%), the 2-year yield would equal 3% (2% + 1%).

The rate expectations viewpoint can be thought of as the "efficient markets hypothesis" as applied to bonds. (Market efficiency is discussed further in Section 4.4.) The idea can be subjected to various statistical tests. For example, the paper "The Empirics of Long-Term US Interest Rates," by Tanweer Akram, and Hiuqing Li, offers statistical analysis that supports the belief that the short-term rate explains the level of long-term bond yields in the United States.

Bond investors use the related concept of forward rates to decide which parts of the yield curve are expensive or cheap. Analysts calculate forward rates using yield curve models, and they

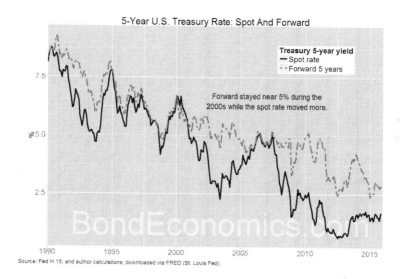

5-Year U.S. Treasury Rate: Spot And Forward

Treasury 5-year yield
— Spot rate
- - Forward 5 years

Forward stayed near 5% during the
2000s while the spot rate moved more.

indicate how the market is pricing the future path of interest rates. For example, a common forward to look at is the 5-year rate, starting 5 years in the future. Normally, the 5-year rate follows the current policy rate quite closely, since business cycles are normally found to last less than 5 years. The 5-year/5-year forward tells us what that rate is discounted to be 5 years from now, which is presumably after current cyclical conditions subside. Since we have little reason to have confidence in 5-year economic forecasts, the working assumption has to be that the forward rate should stick near some "equilibrium" value. If it is "too high" (or "too low"), it is probably a sign that the bond market is cheap (or expensive, respectively). As the chart above illustrates, the 5-year rate, 5 years forward, was relatively stable near 5% during the 2000s, while the spot 5-year rate rose and fell in line with the policy rate. (In the other decades depicted, the forward rate is following the secular downtrend in the policy rate.)

One way of using Taylor Rules as a fixed income analyst is to create forecasts for the underlying variables, and then use a Taylor Rule to generate the path of the policy rate. You then take the average of the policy rate over various terms, and you end up with a "fair value" yield curve.

The existence of term premia muddies the analytical water. If there is a large term premium, a bond yield might bear no resemblance to what anyone expects to happen to the policy rate. In such a case, you can only hope to make money trading bonds by being able to forecast the risk premium – and there is no reason to expect that such a feat is possible.

In a move that should surprise no one, academics in finance and economics have seized upon a complicated mathematical technique for yield curve modelling – without asking whether the results make any sense. Affine term structure models – which are simulations of the evolution of expected interest rates and term premia – are constructed in such a fashion so that rate expectations are largely stable. The implication is that term premia have to move in a high frequency manner ("noisy") in order to replicate the high frequency dynamics of market data. That is, when we see the 10-year note yield rise 20 basis points after a Nonfarm payrolls report, the implication is that the term premium rose by (about) 20 basis points, and the expected path for the policy rate did not change.

Arguing that bond yield movements largely reflect changes in term premia is an internally consistent position. That is, it cannot be proven incorrect. However, it leads to an analytical dead end – we have no hope of explaining the cycles in bond yields. Since I am writing a text discussing interest rate cycles, I have no choice but to choose an alternative coherent position – term premia are small and stable. The implication is that changes in market yields largely reflect shifts in the expected path for the policy rate.

Other factors can reasonably cause term premia to be unstable. The first is the possibility of default by the issuer. This was one of the underlying themes of *Understanding Government Finance*, and I will summarise the argument by saying that default risk is minimal, and should not affect bond pricing in the countries that I am discussing here. (The exception to keep in mind once again is the euro area.) A second factor that could cause the term premium to be unstable is that supply and demand trends could affect bond pricing. For example, increasing amounts of debt could raise term premia. This is a more difficult topic, but I will just assert that the effect would have to be small to be consistent with observed yield curves. The Japanese experience of "high" debt-to-GDP ratios coexisting with low nominal yields tells us that term premia cannot be too sensitive to debt ratios.

4.3 The Yield Curve and the Cycle

The slope of the yield curve is a topic of wide interest in bond market economics. It can be viewed as an economic indicator, or an instrument to be traded. Within this report, the focus is on how and why yield curve slopes act as economic indicators. The advent of ultra-low interest rates has made some interpretations of the yield curve untenable, but the yield curve is still useful as an indicator.

The yield curve is properly the set of all yields for all maturities at a given time. The shortest maturity is overnight, and the longest depends upon the market. The yield curves, in most developed countries, are defined at least to 30-year maturity, but in some cases, yield curve fittings will create a fair value estimate for the yield up to infinite maturity (perpetual bonds). (Perpetual bonds, known as *consols,* are rare as traded instruments, but show up in theoretical work. It is easier to track a single stock of perpetual bonds than a group of bonds with staggered maturity dates.) The curve is either fitted from a set of bonds, or based on swaps, for which there are price quotes at standard maturities.

Dealing with this entire yield curve is difficult; at any given time, it takes a lot of information to specify one. Any specification that uses less than ten parameters will probably not fit most curves very well. That is, we would need ten or more time series to specify the time history of a yield curve. Instead, economists prefer to work with a specification that reduces the amount of information required, which is to take the difference in yield between two fixed maturities – the yield curve slope. By convention, we subtract the yield of the short maturity from the long maturity. For example, the 2-/10-year slope is defined as:

2-/10-year slope = (10-year yield) – (2-year yield).

Yield curves tend to fall into a number of relatively standard shapes. If we choose a sensible short and long maturity point for our slope calculation, the odds are that we can infer how the rest of the curve looks. This section will discuss the 2-year/10-year slope, which is standard, and probably tells us the most about the stance of monetary policy. (Other slopes are only of interest for fixed income relative value trading, such as the slope between 20-year and 30-year bonds.)

A standard piece of terminology refers to the sign of the slope as an economic variable: whether it is positively or negatively sloped.

- A *positive slope* (or *upward-sloping curve*) is a yield curve in which the long maturity is at a higher yield than the short maturity. This is considered a "normal" yield curve state.

- A *negative slope* (or *inverted yield curve*) results when the long maturity yield is less than the short maturity yield. This is relatively rare for standard slopes, and is usually taken as a sign of an imminent recession (for reasons to be discussed below).

The chart below shows the history of the 2-/10-year Treasury slope, along with NBER-defined recessions. We see that the curve inverted solely ahead of recessions. This track history has meant that the 2-/10-year and similar slopes have been used as components of leading economic indicators, or for recession-prediction models.

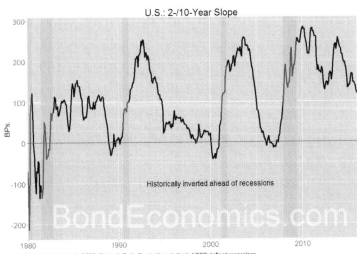

U.S.: 2-/10-Year Slope

Source: Fed H.15, downloaded via FRED (St. Louis Fed). Shaded bars indicate NBER-defined recessions.

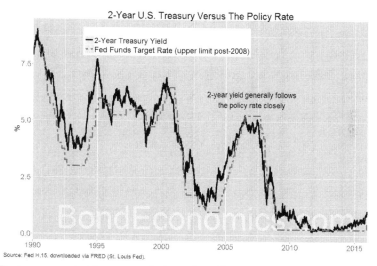

2-Year U.S. Treasury Versus The Policy Rate

Source: Fed H.15. downloaded via FRED (St. Louis Fed).

Rate expectations explain why the 2-/10-year slope works as an indicator.

The short maturity leg (the 2-year yield) is very closely tied to the current level of the policy rate and the expectations for that rate over the coming two years. The chart above demonstrates how the 2-year yield tracked the policy rate, although with some periods of divergence (notably during the 1994 bond bear market). The central bank will quite often move the policy rate to what the market feels is an "extreme" level in order to stimulate or slow the economy, and the 2-year will follow the policy rate.

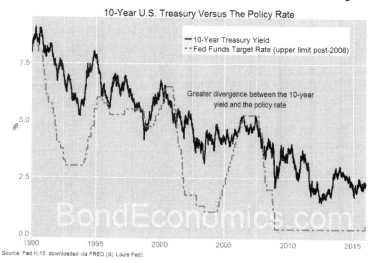

10-Year U.S. Treasury Versus The Policy Rate

Source: Fed H.15. downloaded via FRED (St. Louis Fed).

Meanwhile, the long maturity leg (the 10-year yield) represents the average policy rate over a much longer period. Nobody has any reason to have a detailed economic forecast over such a long period. Instead, the market will tend to keep the expected average of the policy rate starting several years forward near a "neutral" level. (Additionally, the 10-year would presumably have a greater term premium than a 2-year, dragging the long leg's yield higher than the short leg's.) The chart on the previous page demonstrates the tendency of the 10-year yield to diverge from the policy rate (particularly when compared to the 2-year yield).

Taken together, the 2-year yield moves along with the current stance of policy, while the 10-year yield tends to show greater stability. As a result, when the central bank has cut rates and is keeping policy "easy," the yield curve has a positive slope. Conversely, if the economy is heading into recession, the central bank is generally one of the last entities to react. Short maturity yields remain elevated near the current policy rate, while the long maturities plunge as they move to price in the need for extensive rate cuts.

This means that the central bank's reaction function is an important component of slope behaviour. If the central bank was consistently forecasting economic growth better than the markets, and so was able to avoid recessions, there would be no reason to expect that the slope would have any forecasting power. It would largely just reflect the play of risk premia in the bond market.

The advent of ultra-low rates complicates the picture slightly. So long as the markets view deeply negative interest rates as unlikely (Section 2.8), there is an upward bias to rate expectations when the policy rate is near zero. If the economy does not grow, rates will be stuck near zero (as in Japan). However, if the economy starts to grow again, rates can only go up. This explains the generally persistent positive slope in Japan, as seen in the chart on the next page. Nevertheless, the Japanese bond curve has recently allowed for a negative 10-year yield, which does increase the possibility that the yield curve could move more symmetrically.

Although other slopes are likely to remain correlated with the 2-/10-year slope, the relationships become less clear once

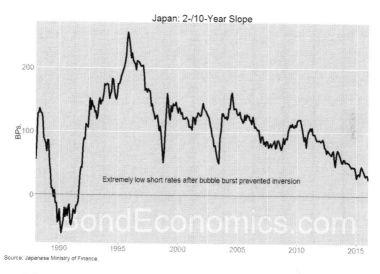

Japan: 2-/10-Year Slope

Extremely low short rates after bubble burst prevented inversion

Source: Japanese Ministry of Finance.

maturities start to lengthen. For example, the slope between a 20-year and 30-year tells us almost nothing about monetary policy, rather it tells us about term premia in the long end of the yield curve. Those long end slopes are of interest for relative value trades, but not for economic analysis.

Finally, the introduction of default risk changes how slopes operate. If an issuer is about to default, all bonds will tend to trade near the expected recovery value, regardless of the bond maturity. This creates an inverted yield curve. Some commentators incorrectly draw this analogy when a government yield curve inverts. So long as the yields are well below 20% (at which point the usual convention is to stop quoting bond yields, and only quote bond prices), a long maturity yield trading below a short maturity yield tells us little about default risk.

The slope tends to move in the opposite direction of the policy rate. This is a factor limiting the effect of the policy rate upon the economy. If the central bank cuts rates rapidly, the slope of the curve can be quite positive. As a result, borrowers who want to lock in a longer term of interest, such as in most fixed mortgages in the United States, will not see as low a rate as is implied by the overnight rate. Conversely, term interest rates can fall during a rate hike cycle, which reduces the ability of the central bank to dampen activity. This was seen as an issue during the rate hike cycle of the 2000s, as discussed in the next section.

4.4 Rate Hike Cycles and Bond Bear Markets

The belief that bond yields reflect the expected path of short rates is equivalent to saying that the bond market is *efficient*. The use of the term efficient is somewhat unfortunate, as saying that something is efficient is often interpreted as saying that it is "good." Furthermore, there is an academic debate about various notions of "market efficiency." In my case, I just use the term as a short-hand meaning that it is difficult to outperform the market as a trader (which is a view normally described as "weak efficiency"). Depending upon the context, the bond market can be viewed as efficient or inefficient. However, from a macro perspective, there do seem to be patterns of inefficiency across the interest rate cycle. Since these cycles are so long (currently around a decade), unfortunately, we have a very small statistical sample to work with. In particular, there are patterns of inefficient behaviour that we see around rate hike cycles.

At the micro level, there are pockets of inefficiency within the fixed income market. These are the stock-in-trade of fixed income relative value analysis. The fixed income markets are used for wholesale funding, and those patterns of funding can create what appears to be either a mispricing or abnormally high risk premia. However, such inefficiencies typically occur in obscure niches of the market, and are not studied by academics.

The main area in fixed income studied by academics is *directional trading* or *market timing* – the ability to make money betting on the short-term direction of interest rates. The message is that it is extremely difficult to make money by timing short-term moves in bond yields. (In bond market jargon, this also would be referred to as "duration trading.")

That said, there does appear to be patterns of the bond market not correctly pricing risks at certain points of the cycle, such as the beginning of a rate hike cycle. Since rate hike cycles are now happening roughly once a decade, there is not a whole lot of statistical evidence either way.

If the bond market were perfectly efficient, sustained bear markets would not exist. Instead, markets would very rapidly jump to new levels in response to new economic data (which would change the outlook for the path of the policy rate), and the movements would otherwise appear to be random. However, sustained bond bear markets do exist (although those bear markets have a shorter lifetime than bond bull markets).

In recent cycles, we have seen a pattern of the bear market occurring earlier relative to the date of the first rate hike. That is a sign of increasing efficiency, but it is still not exactly a random walk. The rest of this section illustrates this pattern. The chart below shows the brutal 1994 bond bear market. What we see is that the 10-year yield started rising only when the Fed started its campaign of rate hikes. Moreover, the pace of the rate hikes was irregular, which possibly kept the market off balance relative to the later cycles. The key is that the bond market did not correctly anticipate the extent of the rise in the short rate, and the correction of expectations only started after the Fed moved. That is, the bond market was reacting to the news of the Fed rate hikes and not purely anticipating Fed actions. If the bond market were perfectly efficient, the 10-year yield should have been higher before the first rate hike, and only oscillating

10-Year Bond Yield And The Policy Rate: 1994 Cycle

Vertical line indicates start of rate hike cycle. Source: Fed H.15, downloaded via FRED (St. Louis Fed).

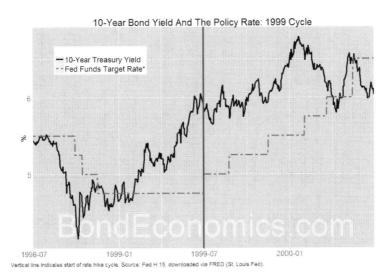

10-Year Bond Yield And The Policy Rate: 1999 Cycle

Vertical line indicates start of rate hike cycle. Source: Fed H.15, downloaded via FRED (St. Louis Fed).

around that higher level as new economic data came in. (Please note that there is a mechanical effect causing yields to rise in response to a steady increase in the policy rate. This mechanical effect is very large for short-maturity bonds, such as a 2-year bond. In such a case, we need to compare bond yields to forward rates to judge how well the market anticipated a rate hike cycle. Such a chart can be difficult to interpret. However, for the 10-year bond yield series that I show here, the forward rate is sufficiently close to the (spot) yield that it is safe to look at the yield.)

The chart for the 1999 cycle (above) shows a slightly different reaction; the market did a better job of anticipating the rate hike cycle. The chart starts with the rate cuts and the plunge in bond yields in 1998. This bond rally was a reaction to the chaos unleashed by the LTCM crisis. In that crisis, the LTCM hedge fund ran into difficulties, as did a large number of other fixed income quantitative traders. These trading desks were forced to unwind spread trades, leading to forced purchases of Treasury bonds, leading to a vicious drop in yields. Meanwhile, the Fed cut rates in response to market turmoil (the so-called "Greenspan Put"), which did lower rate expectations. Nevertheless, once it was clear that the market disruption was contained, the Treasury market lost its flight-to-quality premium, and sold off. This

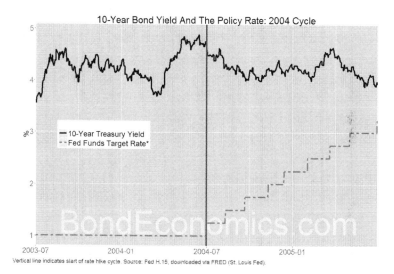

10-Year Bond Yield And The Policy Rate: 2004 Cycle

Vertical line indicates start of rate hike cycle. Source: Fed H.15, downloaded via FRED (St. Louis Fed).

was the first leg of the bond bear market of early 1999. Yields stabilised for a short period at just above 5%, and then the second leg of the bear market occurred, driving the 10-year yield to around 6%. Yields actually stabilised at the time of the first hike; it was only in late 1999 (when technology stocks were peaking) that the last leg of the bear market drove the 10-year closer to 7%.

This cycle illustrates the bond market showing more forward-looking behaviour. The sell-off started ahead of the first rate hike, and one could have argued that the bond market had correctly anticipated the initial expected path of the policy rate. The unexpected strength of the equity market was new information, and so the last leg of the sell-off represented a reaction to that new information. Nevertheless, the pattern of yield movements is following a trend, and does not appear to be a random walk. This implies that there is some form of inertia in rate expectations.

The rate hike cycle starting on June 30, 2004 (chart above) had a bond market reaction that surprised onlookers. The bear market in bonds started roughly three months ahead of the first rate hike, and yields actually fell during the first year of the tightening cycle. This was referred to as a "Conundrum" by Fed Reserve Chairman Alan Greenspan in 2005, and there were many explanations advanced to explain the unwillingness of bond yields to rise in step with the policy rate. (The article by Daniel L. Thornton "Greenspan's Conundrum and the Fed's Ability to Affect Long-Term Yields" analyses this episode.) However, this should be viewed as a sign of the market being somewhat more efficient. More than three months ahead of the first rate hike, the market did not correctly price the rise in short rates. Once it was clear that rates would rise, the market moved to price in the hike cycle. Afterwards, yields drifted in a trading range, as they were hit by incoming economic data.

The post-hike reaction is exactly what we should expect if the bond market is efficient. The only pocket of inefficiency that remains is the fact that there was a steady bear market starting ahead of the cycle. It appears that bond market participants waited to reprice yields higher only once it was clear that everyone else has accepted that a near term rate hike cycle was inevitable.

One may note how rates were raised at a steady 25 basis points per meeting, as opposed to the somewhat random hikes during the 1994 cycle. I discussed the argument about "gradualism" (a policy of consistent 25 basis point rate hikes) in Section 3.5. As was discussed there, gradualism should only affect the front of the curve (where there is less uncertainty about the path of rate hikes). Once we are looking at 10-year yields, reducing the uncertainty around the next few policy rate meetings has limited effect on market pricing.

10-Year Bond Yield And The Policy Rate: 2015 Cycle (To Date)

Vertical line indicates start of rate hike cycle. Source: Fed H.15, downloaded via FRED (St. Louis Fed).

Finally, the current rate hike "cycle" is somewhat of an anomaly. (At the time of writing, there was only a single rate hike, which occurred in December 2015.) Once again, the rate hike was greeted by a rally in bond yields. We need to go back to mid-2013 to see any form of a bond bear market, more than two years ahead of the first rate hike. That bear market was one of few bond bear markets that appear almost unrelated to rate hikes; the sell-off instead reflected the market's disappointment at the reduction of Federal Reserve bond purchases (known as "The Taper Tantrum"). Since a single rate hike hardly counts as a "cycle," it is too early to be surprised by the lack of bond market reaction. If economic growth remains on track, rates could be raised at a less lethargic pace, which would put bond yields under upward pressure.

4.5 Inflation-Linked Bonds

Inflation-linked bonds are a relatively new form of bond (although bonds linked to other prices, such as gold-linked bonds, have a long history). The United Kingdom introduced the bonds in 1981. These bonds are also called "index-linked" bonds, or even "linkers." A full discussion of how these bonds are priced is beyond the scope of this report, but one can use them to infer the expected path of inflation – known as breakeven inflation.

Definition *Breakeven inflation* is the difference between the quoted yield on a conventional bond ("nominal yield") and the quoted yield on an inflation-linked bond of the same maturity ("indexed yield" or "real yield").

For example, if the 10-year nominal yield was 4%, and the 10-year inflation linked bond yield was 2%, the 10-year breakeven inflation rate is 2% (4% -2%). We can say that the bond market is "pricing in" a 2% inflation rate over the next 10 years, as the two bonds would have (roughly) the same total return over the 10-year horizon if the inflation rate were a steady 2% over that period.

This definition of breakeven inflation is only an approximation of the "economic breakeven" between a nominal and inflation-linked bond (that is, what rate of inflation is required for the two bonds to have the same total return?). The approximation will

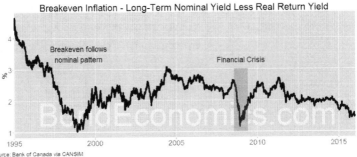

break down for very short maturities, or under other unusual conditions (particularly for individual bonds). However, this approximation is quite close to the economic breakeven if one is working with fitted bond yields (such as the yield series in the Federal Reserve H.15 Report, which are the yield series used in this report).

The initial structure used by the United Kingdom was quite complex. Later, the Canadian government created a cleaner design in the early 1990s – Real Return Bonds. Other countries followed the Canadian model, such as the United States TIPS bonds. Unfortunately, the publicly available data series for TIPS is quite short – only starting in 2003. Since there was only one full cycle during that time (unless the U.S. economy has entered recession), it is difficult to discuss how interest rate cycles relate to breakeven inflation with that data. Instead, we will switch to the Canadian data – for 30-year Real Return Bonds. For these bonds, we have a data set (from the Bank of Canada) stretching back to 1995, which gives us a bit longer track record to look at.

The chart above shows the last two decades of the secular bond bull market in Canada. The top panel shows the *nominal yield* (the yield on a conventional bond), and the *real yield* – the quoted yield on Real Return Bonds. (*Indexed yield* is probably a better term for this rather than real yield, but most people call it the real yield, and I will follow that convention here.)

The second panel shows the difference between the two yields – the breakeven inflation rate. (As a technical note, I am using a "Long-Term Bond Yield" instead of a 30-year benchmark yield for the nominal rate due to data availability issues.)

The experience during the LTCM crisis in 1998 illustrates the directionality effect. As highlighted on the chart, the nominal bond yield fell as that financial crisis took hold, and then reversed higher once it was clear that the U.S. economy was largely going to be unscathed. The technology boom was still under way, and yields rose as the job market tightened and investment boomed.

However, the real yield was largely unchanged during this episode. As a result, the breakeven inflation rate fell then rose, following the pattern of nominal yields (as noted on the chart).

This is part of a familiar pattern for the index-linked market – real yields generally move by less than nominal yields, although they might move in the same direction. That is, the sensitivity of real yield changes to changes in the nominal yield is less than 1. Since the breakeven inflation rate is the difference between those variables, it tends to move in the same direction as nominal yields as a result.

The chart below is a scatter plot of the yield changes for nomi-

* Period = 1995 to 2015. Source: Bank of Canada; downloaded via CANSIM.

nal and real yields on a quarterly basis. The analysis uses the lower frequency quarterly series rather than daily series for a reason. Quarterly yield changes reflect the trend movements in yields; daily yield changes tend to bump around in a more random-looking fashion. The trend line implies that for every basis point the nominal yield moves, the real yield moves by 0.46 basis points.

Obviously, the scatter plot is somewhat of a cloud of points, which understates the effectiveness of the relationship. Most of the time, yields are stuck in trading ranges, and so we can end up with the two markets somewhat uncorrelated. However, if we isolate large movements in yields – bond bull or bear markets – we see that real yields consistently move by less than nominal yields during those periods. In other words, you can trade between the markets based on your view of the big underlying trend in yields.

- If you are a bond bull (expect nominal yields to go down), you buy nominal bonds, and sell index-linked bonds. If you are right, the nominal yield will fall by more than the real yield, and the breakeven inflation rate will drop.
- If you are a bond bear (expect nominal yields to go up), you buy inflation-linked bonds, and sell nominal bonds. If you are right, the nominal yield will rise by more than the real yield, and the breakeven inflation rate will rise.

However, there are limits to how far this directionality will work. Breakeven inflation cannot move too far from expectations, and in the modern era, those expectations have not strayed too far from the central bank's target. The next chart shows the Canadian experience, which is a poster child for inflation targeting. The shaded bar indicates the 1%-3% range for inflation, and the line indicates headline inflation. (Inflation-linked bonds pay off based on headline inflation, which includes food and energy. Economists often prefer to look at core inflation, which excludes those components.) Other than brief misses – generally due to energy price movements – inflation has been within the target band. This helped to anchor 30-year breakeven inflation expectations in the 2%-3% range over most of the period after the year 2000. This anchoring implies that breakeven inflation will

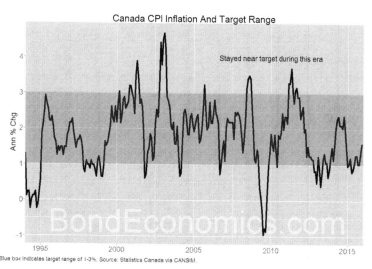

Canada CPI Inflation And Target Range

Stayed near target during this era

Blue box indicates target range of 1-3%. Source: Statistics Canada via CANSIM.

drift within a trading range near the central bank inflation target (assuming that the target remains cred-
ible); the directionality effect explains whether the breakeven will be near the top or the bottom of the trading range.

As stated earlier, this pattern of behaviour has generally held
across the developed countries. The chart below shows the scatter
diagram for yield changes for 10-year U.S. bonds over the 2003-
2015 period. The regression coefficient is slightly higher, with a
sensitivity of 0.53. Once again, this is close to the rule of thumb
that states that real yields move half as much as nominal yields.

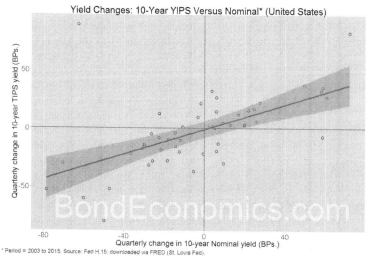

Yield Changes: 10-Year YIPS Versus Nominal* (United States)

* Period = 2003 to 2015. Source: Fed H.15; downloaded via FRED (St. Louis Fed).

Risk premia complicate the analysis of market expectations for inflation. This has been a fertile field of study, with complex affine term structure models used to extract the "true" market expectations for inflation.

I have reservations concerning the methodology to calculate risk premia, but I recognise that there are times when they matter. If you return to my earlier chart of Canadian breakeven inflation, one can note the behaviour during the 2008 Financial Crisis. At that time, nominal yields fell and real yields rose, causing a spectacular plunge in breakeven inflation.

It must be remembered that oil prices did crater after spiking to $150/barrel; but the effect of that deflation is not going to be too significant for 30-year annualised inflation. (Short-term breakeven inflation rates would legitimately be quite negative.) Additionally, the disarray in the financial markets did hit economic confidence, but probably not by as much as the fall in breakeven inflation implied.

The explanation for the move had nothing to do with efficient markets: there were a lot of trading desks stuck in levered positions in index-linked bonds across the developed world. Everybody knew that they had to get out, and nobody who had the capacity to buy was willing to do those other players any favours by paying reasonable prices for index-linked bonds.

None of this has anything to do with stories about "inflation risk premia"; this was just a period when the markets were completely disorderly, and instruments were not priced anywhere near fair value. Very simply, I see no way of modelling such behaviour – how can a mathematical model pinpoint an utterly nonsensical price?

For further reading about inflation-linked bonds, one useful reference for fixed income investors is *Inflation Risks and Products: The Complete Guide* (edited by Brice Benaben and Sébastien Goldenberg). It discusses the inflation-linked markets, as well as how they fit into investors' portfolios. One drawback of the book is that it was published in 2008, and thus cannot address the difficulties the market faced during the Financial Crisis.

4.6 Interest Rates and the Currency

One of the mechanisms by which monetary policy affects the economy is via the value of the currency. Currency values have a direct effect on the competitiveness of exporters in different countries, and so there can be a direct linkage to economic activity. In some cases, the primary effect of the policy rate seems to be felt via the effect on the currency, as the direct impact of interest rates on the domestic can often be limited.

If all goods were traded across borders, we could use cross-border prices to come up with a fair value for a currency. This is what "purchasing power parity" theories revolve around; the best-known example is the Economist's Big Mac™ Index. (That index compares the price of a hamburger across different countries, and is described further at: http://www.economist.com/content/big-mac-index.) However, anyone familiar with purchasing power analysis will be aware that a currency can swing in a wide range around the predicted "fair value."

We need to develop some theory that explains why currencies can vary from what purchasing power parity suggests, which we could term "supply and demand." Within the currency market, we can observe two sectors tugging supply and demand.

- The real economy – how are exports and imports balanced?
- Capital flows. These flows can be broken down into direct investment (including takeovers), fixed income, and equity flows.

In my view, in the developed markets, flows in risk assets (equity markets and takeovers) are the most important determinant of currency levels. Developed countries can routinely run large trade (or current account) deficits without causing the currency to move, whereas very few countries can have their equity markets underperform and have a strong currency. (Japan would appear to be an exception to that rule, but in this case, the value of the Japanese yen is driven by how Japanese investors position their large foreign currency portfolios.)

If we turn to how the policy rate affects the currency, the usual rule-of-thumb is that a higher policy rate will tend to increase the value of a currency ("all else equal").

Within a currency peg regime, such as the Gold Exchange Standard that prevailed during the 1920s, this is logical. If you peg your currency to that of another country, investors may believe that the difference in the bond's returns will be equal to the yield difference: there is no currency risk between the bonds. A higher local interest rate makes your bonds more attractive, and so they should attract capital flows. This will help your currency keep its strength versus its peg (currencies moved within small bands around a desired parity).

It is less clear as to why an interest rate hike would increase the value of a floating currency. Experienced investors know that they cannot safely compare bonds that trade in two different floating currencies based on their yield. However, the rule of thumb is defensible if we take a realistic view about central bank reaction functions.

(Readers familiar with the academic literature will be aware of the concept of *covered interest rate parity*. Interest rate parity is just an arbitrage relationship that determines the ratio of a forward currency rate to the spot rate; it tells us nothing useful about the level of the currency. Some researchers have attempted to use this arbitrage relationship to extract information about the level of the currency, an effort that is misguided. Given the complexity of the topic, it is not addressed here.)

Central banks attempt to forecast activity, and set the policy rate based upon their forecasts. Although the central bank may have only a questionable ability to forecast what is going to happen in 1-2 years, it still has enough resources to have a better idea about current activity than is the case for any particular market participant. Therefore, one could argue that the central bank acts as a referee to give the "best" estimate of the current state of the economy (although they have problems with recession forecasting, like everybody else).

Therefore, a central bank that is confident enough to raise rates provides a good quality signal that the prospects are tilted towards faster nominal growth. In an environment with un-hinged inflation expectations (such as in the 1970s), that might not be a good thing for financial assets. However, in the post-1990s environment with stable inflation rates, higher nominal activity generally coincides with stronger real growth. This growth attracts investors in risky assets (including corporate mergers and acquisition activity), which buoys the currency.

The figure below gives an example of how complicated this can be.

The top panel shows the Canadian dollar versus the U.S. dollar; the quote convention is that a higher value is a weaker Canadian dollar. The bottom panel shows the 5-year government bond yields. (We need to look at both sets of interest rates, as a currency price is a relative price, and what matters is the spread of interest rates.) We can see very considerable swings in the currency; one could attempt to line them up with what

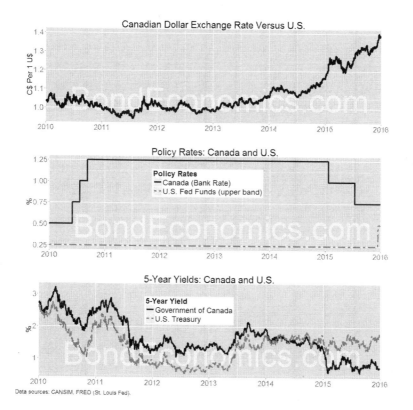

Data sources: CANSIM, FRED (St. Louis Fed).

is happening with relative interest rates, but it is difficult to do.

If we just look at the end of the data set, we see that it is conforming to the rule-of-thumb I gave above. Although the U.S. policy rate is still below that of Canada, the weakness in the Canadian economy has led the 5-year Government of Canada yield to drop below that of the 5-year Treasury. The Fed was expected to raise rates slowly, while the Bank of Canada was expected to keep rates unchanged or even lower them. At the same time, the Canadian dollar has weakened. The interest rate signal is pointing in the same direction as the signal from the real economy, and the relative attractiveness of Canadian corporate assets. (The value of the Canadian equity market was largely dominated by commodity firms, and so commodity weakness provides an incentive for outflows out of Canadian stocks.) This is also aligned with trade trends, as the value of Canadian energy exports collapsed.

This example shows that we cannot easily disentangle the real economy effects from the financial market effects. Once again, policy rate trends may tend to lead this process, but that can be attributed to central banks accurately gauging current conditions. This means that statistical tests could signal that policy rate spreads "cause" currency moves. Although true, this usage of the word "cause" should not be mistaken for the common sense interpretation of the word, which would imply a cause-and-effect mechanism. In my view, the capital flows are the driving mechanism, and policy rate spreads are correlated with those flows.

Chapter 5 The Analytical Challenge of Recessions

5.1 Introduction

Recession timing represents the most difficult and most important task for economic forecasters. Recessions are costly for societies, and typically create large market movements. Half of the interest rate cycle (when rates are cut) is entirely driven by the event of a recession. Unfortunately, as shall be seen in Section 5.2, the consensus opinion of economists has reliably been unable to forecast these events. Economists have had better luck in other forecasting exercises.

- During an expansion, GDP growth rates tend to be steady, courtesy of the effect of various automatic stabilisers embedded within modern economies. These stabilisers include well-known effects of the welfare state (as people lose employment, they receive unemployment insurance payments, and they stop having income and payroll taxes withheld), as well as some stabilising mechanics within the private sector. For example, imports are reduced as demand falls, causing the external balance to move in a direction favourable for growth ("all else equal"). This means that economists have a reasonable chance to forecast GDP growth outside of recessions.

- It is possible to take advantage of the known properties of other economic series in order to make short-term forecasts. For example, one can attempt to forecast the Consumer Price Index (CPI) by using knowledge about its components. In the United States, one of the largest components of the CPI is Owner's Equivalent Rent, and that time series is smoothed by construction. This smoothing creates a steady momentum in the inflation rate for that component, making it easy to forecast a few periods ahead. Meanwhile, the most volatile component of the CPI is gasoline prices, for which average prices are available in real time on a weekly or even daily basis. As a result, it is relatively straightforward to forecast the upcoming CPI number.

The creation of "recession indicators" has been a major area of economic research. Such indicators seem to offer a quantitative measure of the odds of the economy falling into recession. Although this work is interesting, I am cautious about the results, for reasons that are discussed in this chapter. Section 5.3 outlines the fundamental factors that cause a recession, and they will vary greatly from cycle to cycle, making the creation of a composite recession indicator difficult. Since modern recessions have been spaced about a decade apart, the test sample size is necessarily small.

5.2 The Consensus and Recessions

One of the more entertaining robust empirical observations in economics is the inability of the economic consensus to forecast recessions. (Since there are a very large number of economists

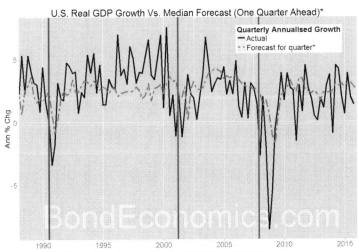

U.S. Real GDP Growth Vs. Median Forecast (One Quarter Ahead)*

* Philadelphia Fed Survey of Professional Forecasters. Vertical lines indicate NBER recession starts (monthly).

making all manner of economic predictions, one common strategy is to take an average of economist forecasts. This average is referred to as "the consensus.") As shown in the chart on the previous page, the median forecast for the quarter-ahead real GDP growth rate was just above 2% in each of the three last recessions. (The survey used was the data from the "Survey of Professional Forecasters" recorded by the Philadelphia Federal Reserve.) In the chart, the vertical lines indicate the monthly start dates of recessions (as determined by the NBER recession dating committee), while the time series are for quarterly annualised real GDP growth. The forecast series is shifted to correspond to the date of the forecast; for example, the value of the survey taken in the fourth quarter of 2014 is plotted in the first quarter of 2015.

The chart focuses on the start of the recession, as the remainder of the recession is obviously a greater challenge for forecasting. There is typically a V-shaped recovery in growth once the recovery starts, and the economy will typically regain a large percentage of the lost growth. Forecasting the growth rate in the recovery is nearly impossible, since we do not have reliable estimates of the extent of the downturn in real time.

For the other non-recessionary periods, I would not be particularly concerned about the accuracy of the median forecast. The survey forecasts were based on real GDP as was reported at the time, whereas the historical series shown takes into account revisions to the data. There are one-time effects in GDP estimates that reliably reverse themselves, and so one-period ahead forecasts will incorporate such reversions. Meanwhile, the entire blip might be revised out of existence in later versions of the GDP series, and so the forecast reversions no longer correspond to anything in the data.

Although it is entertaining to poke fun at highly paid economists who reliably get the most important forecast wrong, we need to dig deeper. The professional forecasters in the survey are not academics who can stick with failed methodologies because they are protected by academic politics – these professional forecasters are going to use the best forecasting tools available. The implication is that it is very difficult to call the timing of recessions. Since modern cycles end in popped bubbles, it is easy to say, "This will end badly – eventually." However, even patently ridiculous bubbles can avoid popping for a long time. Nevertheless, there is also an underlying hopeful message for analysts. You do not need to have a "good" forecast; you just need a "less bad" forecast than the consensus. In the Financial Crisis, it was not that hard to realise that the global economy was going off the rails before the collapse of Lehman Brothers made that fact clear to everyone.

This inability to time recessions is what post-Keynesian economics predicts. An inability to get recession forecasts right is only an intellectual puzzle to strong believers in *rational expectations* (which imply that private sector activity forecasts that are on average correct). The core of the post-Keynesian argument is straightforward: the future is shrouded in uncertainty, and that uncertainty cannot be reduced to a well-defined probability distribution for future growth.

If we are looking at the accuracy of recession forecasts, central banks get a free pass. Central banks are amongst the best sources for economic forecasts, but they are politically incapable of forecasting recessions. Although I have little patience with theories that state that the central bank can magically push economy variables to desired levels by managing expectations, there is a grain of truth behind that idea. Central banks are regulators, and are privy to a good deal of "inside information" concerning the financial system. Given the linkage between financial crises and recessions, a panicking central bank provides a very good justification for panicking yourself; as a result, there could be self-fulfilling downward spiral in activity. As a result, we have to expect self-censorship concerning recession calls by central bankers.

5.3 Post-Keynesian Economics and Recessions

One of the distinguishing features of both old Keynesian and post-Keynesian economics is the emphasis on economic aggregates and national accounting. By contrast, mainstream economics starts with an emphasis on microeconomic decisions, and only uneasily works its way towards aggregate behaviour. This difference creates quite different views of how the economic cycle evolves.

I will not attempt to give an academic survey of post-Keynesian thought here. Instead, I will give my interpretation of the work of Hyman Minsky (which is directly rooted in the theories of Keynes and Michal Kalecki).

The key building block for the analysis is the Kalecki Profit Equation (although Jerome Levy developed a very similar idea in parallel). This equation is based on national accounting identities, and explains the sources of aggregate business sector profits. Using simplified national accounting concepts, we can say:

Profits = Net Investment + Dividends − Fiscal Surplus − Trade Deficit − Household Savings.

Rather than attempt a derivation here, I will instead explain why this result holds. (Please note that the full version of this equation will include more terms, in order to take into account some of the complications in the national accounts, such as the effect of foreign aid transfers.) If we look at the business sector in aggregate, we will see cash flowing in and out to the other sectors in a circular fashion. For our simplified accounting system, the cash inflows are generally business revenue, and *most* outflows are an expense. Profit is the revenues less the expenses.

Importantly, the wage bill does not feature in the profit equation. This may not match intuition, as the wage bill is the largest expense of an individual firm. This is the result of the notion of circular flows of money. If a firm pays its workers $1000, and those workers do not save any of it, the implication is that they are immediately buying $1000 in goods and services from the business sector. The net result for aggregate profits is nil, since the wage expense of $1000 is matched by $1000 in new business revenue (most likely at another firm). Various terms in the profit equation are the result of the breakage of that circular flow. For example, if workers save money out of their wages, sales to workers are less than their wages, and the result is a loss for the business sector. This is why we need to subtract household savings in the profit equation.

The other two terms that subtract from profits − "fiscal surplus," and "trade deficit" – also represent leaks in the flow of money. (A *fiscal surplus* results if the government sector takes in more taxes than it spends. A *trade deficit* is the case when imports are greater than exports.) If households are a net payer of money to the government, that leaves them less money to consume the output of the business sector. As a result, a fiscal surplus subtracts from aggregate profits. (The typical situation is a fiscal deficit, which increases profits.) A trade deficit also represents a loss to the domestic business sector – the money that goes to the foreign sector is not returning to the domestic business sector.

However, not all monetary outflows from the business sector are expenses. In such a case, if that money returns to the circular flow, it is a net source of profit. The first two terms of the profit equation are these flows. Dividends that are paid out to the household sector are a source of consumption demand like wages, but the payment of a dividend is not an expense.

Net Investment is investment in real assets less depreciation, and is the key driver of the business cycle. (*Depreciation* is an accounting concept. Each year, businesses reduce the value of their fixed assets, and this reduction in value is depreciation. It is an expense, even though there is no associated cash outlay during the current accounting period.) Please note that "investment" as it is used here bears no relationship to the common usage of the word, in which the purchase of financial assets constitutes "investment." Since the purchase of financial assets does not create direct income flow (unlike the investment by firms in assets), we cannot mix up these two definitions of "investment" when discussing national accounting.

Since investment is not (immediately) expensed, these flows do not immediately reduce profits. (Depreciation expenses will occur later, but in a growing economy, new investment will generally be larger than depreciation of the existing capital stock.) Note that investment also includes the buildup of inventories. (When a firm sells something out of existing inventory, this represents a negative investment in inventories, which reduces profits. This matches intuition – the cost of goods sold reduces profit.)

Net investment is the one term within the equation that is un-equivocally pro-cyclical. Investment rises as "animal spirits" in the business sector improve. The other terms tend to dampen an expansion, although dividends have a mixed effect. Dividend payments generally rise during an expansion, but most shareholders have a high saving rate, and so increased household sector savings will probably counteract the dividend increase. During an expansion, the fiscal balance tends to move towards surplus, creating a fiscal drag on profits. If the domestic economy is growing more quickly than foreign ones, the trade balance tends to move towards a deficit during an expansion. Finally, increasing household incomes will probably lead to increased saving out of income. (Housing bubbles, a common occurrence during recent expansions, will lower savings and increase housing investment, as seen in various housing-driven cycles across the developed world.)

Since investment is a major driver of profits, it creates a powerful feedback loop – because businesses invest in response to the expectation of greater profits. Rising investment increases profits, validating earlier decisions to invest. The economy "melts up"; incomes and production follow an unstable exponential growth path. (The tendency to normalise variables by the size of GDP means that people tend to ignore the instability that is implied by exponential growth.) The "automatic stabilisers" within the economy just hold this exponential growth to a reasonable rate.

Of course, this feedback loop works until it doesn't. Eventually, businesses have invested too much, or badly, and the demand for their output that they face is well below their productive capacity. Investment plans are cut, and then the feedback loop works in reverse – falling investment validates fears that profits will fall. Once again, automatic stabilisers come to the rescue. Within the Kalecki Profit Equation, the fiscal balance term invariably blows out to a big deficit, rescuing corporate profits and allowing expansion to resume.

If the investment is largely financed by retained profits, the business sector will be relatively stable, and we might hope to be able to forecast the investment cycle based on standard business cycle indicators (capacity utilisation, profits, etc.). However, as time passes, more and more investment is financed by debt issuance. Moreover, there is an increase in the number of aggressive investors, who have views of the future that are far too optimistic. (Hyman Minsky is the economist most associated with detailing this shift in the quality of borrowing.)

Eventually, the lenders discover that they have been financing a lot of investment that probably should not have taken place. Since modern corporate managements are rewarded handsomely for producing growth – and are penalised little for failure – the borrowers themselves do not curtail their debt-fuelled investment plans. Instead, the plug has to be pulled by the lenders. Unfortunately, the incentives in modern finance are such that investors are not rewarded for acting too quickly, and so the sudden stop in lending typically only comes after something has gone horribly wrong in the wholesale funding markets.

It should be noted that this process of increasing leverage takes time. Modern corporate managers do not like fixed investment; rather the preference is for financial engineering. This means that the bulk of the business sector finances investment out of retained profits, and so it is not subject to the "sudden stop" of financing. This explains why modern expansions last such a long time, relative to the pre-1990s experience. (The reduction of inventories by "just-in-time inventory management," and the secular decline of manufacturing, is another important explanation for lower business cycle volatility. However, the decline of manufacturing and inventories are just other symptoms of the change in management culture.)

The rise of speculative borrowing arises in new sectors, dominated by managers who are focused on growth, and are not particularly concerned by old-school notions about paying back lenders. It takes time for these "growth stories" to emerge, as investors usually spend a couple of years after a recession rebuilding their portfolios and risk-management systems after the previous bust.

With this narrative of the business cycle in place, it is now straightforward to see why it is hard to predict a business sector-led recession. We need to be able to pinpoint the time at which investors are going to rein in their financing of new investment. The timing of this "sudden stop" is not driven by the economic variables tracked by the national statistical agencies – it is driven by the determination of the weak links within the financial sector. If you could easily make such a determination, it would be correspondingly easy to make money in the financial markets. I subscribe to at least a weak version of "market efficiency:" markets may not be perfect forecasting mechanisms, but there are not a whole lot of organisations with a strong track record of timing them.

Finally, one should note that it should be easier to forecast a *policy-induced* recession than one that is the result of private sector activity. For example, the disastrous austerity policies implemented in the euro area periphery (for example, Greece) were widely expected to cause a depression, and that is exactly what happened. Although the possibility of such errors always needs to be kept in mind, most countries generally attempt to avoid running their economies straight into the ground. As a result, the number of examples this type of recession should be limited.

5.4 Oil Price Spikes

One of the interesting regularities of modern American recessions was the linkage between oil price spikes and recession

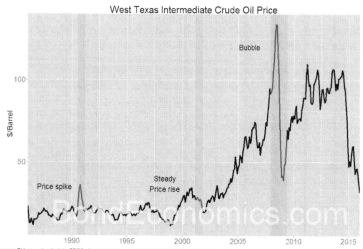

timing. As the previous chart illustrates, rising oil prices preceded all modern American recessions. Since hydrocarbon fuel sources are the major power source of modern economies, there appears to be an obvious mechanical linkage. In fact, some economists have used this linkage to argue that oil prices were the driver of the 2008 downturn. In my view, some of these oil price rises were somewhat coincidental, although an oil price spike may have influenced the exact timing of recession.

(The linkage between oil prices and recessions in countries other than the United States is less clear. This could be explained by the fact that other countries tax gasoline more heavily, and so retail price rises are moderate relative to the rise of wholesale crude prices. The U.S. consumer also uses much more gasoline per year than counterparts do in many other regions.)

There are a number of reasons why oil price spikes could cause recessions.

- Global oil production occurs in a few regions (notably the Middle East). A rise in oil prices acts as a tax on consumers elsewhere, whereas the increased income only boosts activity in the oil-producing regions.
- If the rise in oil prices is rapid, it is extremely unlikely that oil producers will increase their spending by enough to balance their increased income. The rise in savings causes a near-term loss of aggregate demand.
- Energy use is embedded within the entire production chain, and consumers have little ability to substitute away from oil use in the short term. For example, workers who commute by car to their place of work have little choice but to keep filling up their tank. (In the longer term, consumption patterns change to reduce energy use.)
- Anything that disrupts existing patterns of economic activity can cause leveraged businesses to fail, causing lower economic activity.

These factors suggest why we should not be completely surprised by the timing of oil price spikes and recessions. Very simply, if one occurs, a recession always remains a possibility.

However, one could argue that the association between recessions and oil price spikes was coincidental. Modern economic expansions have tended to be global in scope. During these expansions, rising incomes lead to increasing automobile use globally, leading to demand pressures within the oil market. Meanwhile, geologists are no longer finding massive oil fields, slowing production growth. Correspondingly, it is not particularly surprising that oil prices rise during an expansion. As a result, we would always expect oil prices to be highest just when growth has peaked; that is, when a recession hits.

In summary, one needs to keep in mind resource constraints when gauging the outlook for the economic cycle. However, one should be careful in taking too strong a stance that the business cycle *solely* depends upon conditions in the energy market.

5.5 Bubbles and Recessions

Recessions in recent decades have been associated with the aftermath of asset bubbles bursting. This is distinct from the experience in the early decades after World War II, as the financial system was tightly constrained, and there were no financial bubbles of note. Given the somewhat elastic definition of what constitutes a "bubble," it would not be surprising that this association continues.

Broadly speaking, equity bubbles are less dangerous for economies than bubbles driven by debt, which are typically associated with real estate bubbles (both commercial and residential real estate). One justification for that claim is the econometric analysis in the paper "Leveraged Bubbles" by Jordà, Schularick, and Taylor. This paper analyses the effect of bubbles on the severity of recessions.

The first challenge is to define a "bubble," as practically every movement in any asset class ends up labelled as a "bubble" by hyperbolic editors and analysts. The authors used the following criteria to define a bubble (details on page 9 of the referenced paper).

- The price of the asset (in real terms) has to be elevated from its historical trend. This is a period of "overvaluation" (my term, they used "price elevation episode").

(Technically, they used a Hodrick-Prescott filter with $\lambda=100$, and looked for a 1 standard deviation rise above the filtered trend.)

- The real price of the asset has to fall by at least 15% over a 3-year window during this period of "overvaluation." It is not enough for an asset to shoot up in value; also, it has to have a price correction. Therefore, this is not just a question of there being a "bubble," it has to "pop."

(As a technical aside, since they are looking at an asset price relative to its trend, we cannot say that the asset in question was overvalued in absolute terms, only relative to its own history. Furthermore, the technique used cannot be used in "real time," that is, we cannot use it to determine whether a given asset market is experiencing a bubble now. We need to wait years in order to calculate what the "underlying trend" truly is. This is a generic weakness of the Hodrick-Prescott filter, as discussed in Section 2.4 (and in Appendix A.1). The particular problem with the Hodrick-Prescott filter in this instance is that we do not know how long we need to wait until the calculated "trend" will be stable.)

The authors worked with a large data set of 17 countries, with annual data going back to 1870. Since post-World War II data act quite differently than earlier data, they also provided results for the post-World War II data set. If we confine ourselves to that recent data, the experience with recessions is summarised as follows.

- There were 65 recessions not associated with financial crises ("normal recessions"). (Note that if two countries fall into recession at the same time, the event counts as two recessions, even if the two are linked to the same causes.) Of those, 24 recessions did not have either a housing or equity bubble (36.9%).
- There were 23 recessions associated with financial crises, and only 2 of those recessions did not feature asset price bubbles (8.7%).

Since recessions associated with financial crises tend to be deeper than "normal" recessions, it is clear that having an asset bubble is going to be associated with a worse economic outcome.

5.6 Lessons from the 2010 Cycle

The current business cycle illustrates the difficulties with forecasting recessions, at least in most regions. (Various euro area nations drove themselves into depressions in the post-Crisis period as the result of austerity policies.)

If we look at the global economy, we need to discuss Chinese developments. Given that the economies in the developed world are largely stagnant, China has been the major source of global growth. The Chinese economy has confounded skeptics for decades (including myself). The economy is continuing to grow, despite any number of signs of speculative excess, and what can only be described as "mal-investment." These imbalances would have resulted in the business cycle being choked off in Western countries, but the Chinese government has managed to push the economy forward. At the time of writing, Chinese growth has apparently slowed, but it has not produced the "sudden stop" some bearish commentators have forecast. Even if we are not interested in the Chinese economy, it matters for various commodity producers in the developed world (Australia, and to a lesser extent, Canada). This example shows that expertise in analysing private sector activity is not enough to forecast global growth; we also need to take into account the stances of various governments.

Given the inherent difficulty in analysing the possibility of a global recession, this section will just focus on the United States. Since the end of the recession in 2009, GDP growth has been slow, and there have been a number of recession scares. However, growth has returned to a trend growth rate each time. This apparent stability finally led the Fed to raise the policy rate for the first time in December 2015 (and the only hike, at the time of writing).

Although aggregate growth was relatively steady, the sectoral movements were much less placid. The United States had been the centre of a boom in "unconventional" oil production, leading to a boom in shale oil producing regions. When oil prices fell below $100/barrel in 2015, the unconventional producers were no longer able to produce their high-cost oil at a profit.

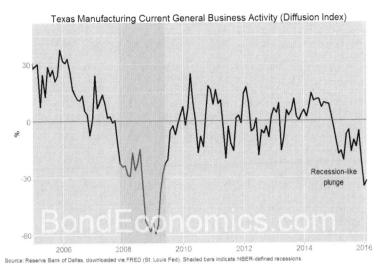

Texas Manufacturing Current General Business Activity (Diffusion Index)

Source: Reserve Bank of Dallas, downloaded via FRED (St. Louis Fed). Shaded bars indicate NBER-defined recessions.

Energy producers were forced to cut back, cutting their activity, and the activity of their suppliers. Since small firms with speculative debt financing dominated unconventional production, various segments of the high yield bond market came under pressure, with many issues trading at distressed prices. As the chart of the survey of business activity in Texas above shows, something that resembled a recession hit the area in 2015.

So far, the national economy has warded off the blow of the energy sector. Although the sector created well-paid jobs, the number of jobs created was small relative to the national economy. Broadly speaking, no matter how bad the situation gets in North Dakota, the impact on the economy of New York City is not going to be that large. At the national level, the service sector drives job growth.

Assuming that the United States can continue to avoid recession, this episode shows the dangers of relying on narratives and arbitrarily selecting various indicators to forecast recessions. The energy boom featured exactly the same sort of loose lending standards and speculative activity that we saw heading into the Financial Crisis. Meanwhile, various sectoral indicators have plunged in exactly the same way one would associate with a recession. However, the weakness in that sector has not been enough to drag the national economy into recession (so far).

In order to gauge the odds of recession properly, one needed to gauge the direct and indirect impact of the sectoral slow-down on the national economy. Since the odds of having a reliable model of the economy with all of the sectors properly specified are low, the only way to do this is via the use of *ad hoc* analysis techniques. Unfortunately, if the implication is that we need to do specialised analysis for each business cycle, it implies that we are unlikely to develop a general-purpose recession forecasting indicator that will work across all cycles.

Chapter 6 Conclusions

6.1 The Interest Rate Cycles of the Future

The modes of analysis within this report give an understanding of the interest rate cycles that occur within a relatively stable economic structure. Inflation expectations largely stick close to the inflation target, and the economy does not deviate too far from previous trends.

Admittedly, the slowdown in the Financial Crisis was relatively violent, and the recovery was only partial in the United States. The labour market has been weak, but to a certain extent, that is just an extrapolation of previous trends, which were only hidden by a temporary construction boom. There has been a great deal of disappointment regarding "Secular Stagnation" since the end of the crisis, but slow growth has been the order of the day for decades. As a result, we could adapt existing models to develop forecasts in the current American economic environment.

Stability is not the order of the day everywhere else. The American post-crisis experience bears no resemblance to the economic disasters that befell Greece and other unfortunate members of the euro area. The meltdown of Greek economic activity is comparable to other economic failures elsewhere, but I doubt that we can hope to fit a model to the data. Although one could try to think in terms of an output gap and inflation expectations, I doubt that the exercise will provide good forecasting results.

The multi-decade bond bull market raises interesting questions. It is not a particularly deep insight at this point to note that there has been a downward trend in the policy rate across the cycles, but we need to ask what could cause the trend to reverse. If we want to believe mainstream economics, perhaps the temporary shocks that reduced growth will abate, and the United States will return to a more robust growth trajectory. Alternatively, political stasis could be broken, and a new policy framework will be embraced that will drive stronger growth.

The current policy consensus has favoured slow growth, and it has been politically robust. Although politicians like to announce plans that will allegedly raise economic growth, they do not want to deal with the inflationary consequences of rising wages. The revealed preference amongst policymakers is for slow growth with low inflation. This political bias has made it safe to bet on growth disappointments and lower interest rates. Nevertheless, it is unsafe to extrapolate the current environment too far into the future. Going forward, fixed income analysts may need to start paying more attention to political trends than the technical musings of central banks.

Appendix

A.1 Multiple Taylor Rule Generation

This appendix expands upon the discussion of Taylor Rules in Section 2.7. As was noted in that section, the difficulty with Taylor Rules is that despite their appearance of scientific impartiality, the choice of rule is essentially arbitrary. This arbitrary nature means that researchers have the ability to find a rule that validates their prior views.

In order to illustrate this, I needed to generate a large number of such rules, and see how this set of rules behaves. It is not enough to come up with completely arbitrary rules, instead, it is necessary to come up with an objective measure whether a rule is "acceptable."

The quantitative metric to decide acceptability used is the "root-mean-squared error" of a Taylor Rule. The deviation of the rule output from the actual policy rate over the 1987-2014 period determines the magnitude of this error.

(The root-mean-squared error is defined as follows.
- Calculate the prediction error at each quarterly data point;
- square these errors;
- calculate the average (mean) of these squared errors;
- take the square root of this average.

This quantifies the magnitude of the fitting error; if the fit were perfect, the root-mean-squared error would be zero.)

I then needed to decide what threshold for the root-mean-squared error marks a rule as being "acceptable." I followed the lead of John Taylor. He admits that the parameter choices he uses in [Taylor 1993] were arbitrary, so I used the root-mean-squared error of a rule that uses his parameters as being my arbitrary cut

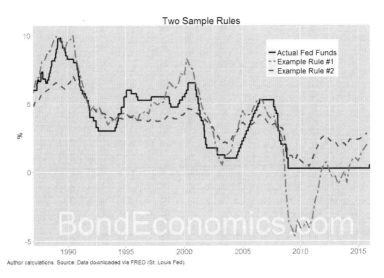

Author calculations. Source: Data downloaded via FRED (St. Louis Fed).

off. In other words, a rule is "acceptable" if it has a root-mean-squared error that is less than or equal to the rule using the parameters of a real rate of 2%, and feedback parameters of (½, ½) on the output gap and inflation expectation terms.

The chart above gives an example of two Taylor Rules compared to the actual Fed Funds. I picked these two rules out of a larger set of "acceptable" rules based on the spread between their predicted values at the endpoint. Although they do not always diverge, there are cases when they are on the opposite

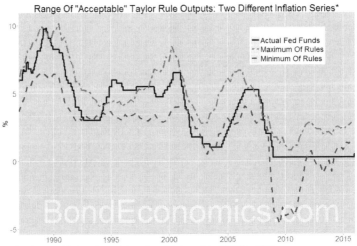

* Uses GDP deflator or core CPI inflation. Author calculations. Source: Data downloaded via FRED (St. Louis Fed).

side of the actual policy rate. An analyst can just look at these time series and decide which one better fits their worldview.

We can go beyond these two rules. The chart at the bottom of the previous page (also shown in Section 2.7) shows the range of possible outputs at each date, based on the entire set of "acceptable" rules.

In order to interpret the previous chart, I want to emphasise that the maximum and minimum values are those achieved on a date by *any* "acceptable" rule. A particular rule will lie between (or on top of) those limits.

The chart below illustrates this by comparing the first example rule versus the limits. This particular rule has high coefficients on the output gap and inflation term, and it swings between the maximum and minimum values. It is clear that by allowing more flexibility to the specification of the Taylor rule (such as allowing for a time-varying natural rate of interest) would allow an even greater ability to pick and choose amongst desired levels for the predicted policy rate.

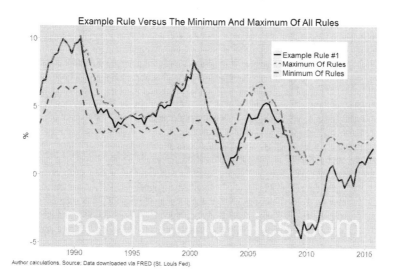

Data Sources

This text relies upon data that has come from a variety of national sources. In some cases, the data are calculated by one agency, but distributed by another. My charts list the data sources used (in abbreviated form). Please note that hyperlinks change over time; you may need to search for updated links.

- **Canada.** Canadian data used was calculated either by Statistics Canada or by the Bank of Canada. All data have been downloaded from the CANSIM delivery platform. URL: http://www5.statcan.gc.ca/cansim/home-accueil?lang=eng&p2=50&HPA

- **United States.** The United States has a number of agencies that generate statistical data. I most commonly use the Bureau of Economic Analysis (BEA) as well as the Bureau of Labor Statistics (BLS). For most of these sources, I download the data from the Federal Reserve Economic Data (FRED) website, which is a service provided by the St. Louis Federal Reserve Bank. (Other sources for U.S. data are noted below.) URL: http://research.stlouisfed.org/fred2/

- **United States Flow of Funds.** This is the Z.1 release, which is calculated by the Board of Governors of the Federal Reserve System. It is a comprehensive database of stocks and flows of financial assets. Given the number of series involved, it is easier to download the entire block of Z.1 data than on a series-by-series basis from FRED. URL: http://www.federalreserve.gov/releases/z1/

- **Philadelphia Federal Reserve's Survey of Professional Forecasters.** A public domain time series of economist forecasts. URL: https://www.philadelphiafed.

org/research-and-data/real-time-center/survey-of-pro-fessional-forecasters/

- **IMF.** The IMF publishes World Economic Outlook (WEO) databases, which contains historical data as well as forecasts. One of the advantages of these data is that the data are presented using a consistent set of national accounting concepts. URL: https://www.imf.org/external/ns/cs.aspx?id=28
- **Japanese Ministry of Finance.** The Ministry of Finance (MoF) has a number of databases, including bond yields. URL: http://www.mof.go.jp/english/jgbs/reference/interest_rate/index.htm

Calculations and plotting are done in the *R* computer language. Plots are generated using the *ggplot2* package.

References and Further Reading

This report is informal and the bibliography has been limited in size. Please note that hyperlinks change over time; you may need to search for updated links.

The reader is also directed to the websites of various central banks, as they contain a mass of material explaining how they view monetary policy. The publications cover a wide range of complexity.

- "The Empirics of Long-Term US Interest Rates," Tanweer Akram, and Huiqing Li. Working Paper No. 863, Levy Economics Institute, March 2016. URL: http://www.levy-institute.org/pubs/wp_863.pdf
- mFilter package (R language), Mehmet Balcilar. Used for the HP filter calculations.
- "The NAIRU in Theory and Practice," Laurence Ball and N. Gregory Mankiw. Journal of Economic Perspectives, Volume 16, Number 4, Pages 115–136, Fall 2002.
- *Inflation Risks and Products: The Complete Guide*. Edited by Brice Benaben and Sébastien Goldenberg. Risk Books, 2008.
- "Gradualism," Ben Bernanke (Board of Governors of the Federal Reserve). Speech given on May 20, 2004. URL: http://www.federalreserve.gov/boarddocs/Speeches/2004/200405202/default.htm
- *The Best Way to Rob a Bank is to Own One: How Corporate Executives and Politicians Looted the S&L Industry*, William K. Black. University of Texas Press, 2005.
- "What Have We Learned since October 1979?" Alan S. Blinder, Princeton University, CEPS Working Paper No. 105, April 2005. URL: https://www.princeton.edu/ceps/

workingpapers/105blinder.pdf
- *Monetary Policy, Inflation, and the Business Cycle: An Introduction to the New Keynesian Framework,* Jordi Galí. Princeton University Press, 2008.
- "Leveraged Bubbles" by Jordà, Ò, M Schularick, and A M Taylor. NBER Working Papers 21486, 2015, URL: http://www.nber.org/papers/w21486
- *Post-Keynesian Economics: New Foundations,* Marc Lavoie. Edward Elgar, 2014.
- *Stabilizing an Unstable Economy,* Hyman Minsky. Mc-Graw-Hill, 2008.
- *Full Employment Abandoned: Shifting Sands and Policy Failures,* William Mitchell and Joan Muysken. Edward Elgar, 2008.
- "Discretion versus policy rules in practice," Professor John B. Taylor of Stanford University, Carnegie-Rochester Series on Public Policy, 39, 1993. URL: http://web.stanford.edu/~johntayl/Papers/Discretion.PDF
- "Greenspan's Conundrum and the Fed's Ability to Affect Long-Term Yields," Daniel L. Thornton, September 2012, St. Louis Fed Working Paper 2012-036A, URL: https://research.stlouisfed.org/wp/2012/2012-036.pdf

About the Author

Brian Romanchuk founded the website BondEconomics.com in 2013. It is a website dedicated to providing analytical tools for the understanding of the bond markets and monetary economics.

He previously was a senior fixed income analyst at *la Caisse de dépôt et placement du Québec*. He held a few positions, including being the head of quantitative analysis for fixed income. He worked there from 2006-2013. Previously, he worked as a quantitative analyst at BCA Research, a Montréal-based economic-financial research consultancy, from 1998-2005. During that period, he developed a number of proprietary models for fixed income analysis, as well as covering the economies of a few developed countries.

Brian received a Ph.D. in Control Systems Engineering from the University of Cambridge, and held post-doctoral positions there and at McGill University. His undergraduate degree was in electrical engineering, from McGill. He is a CFA charter holder.

Brian currently lives in the greater Montréal area.

Also by BondEconomics

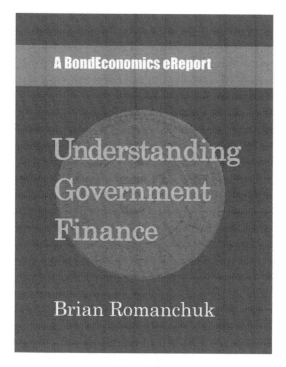

Understanding Government Finance (June 2015)

A government budget is not like a household budget. This report introduces the financial operations used by a central government with a free-floating currency, and explains how they differ from that of a household or corporation. The focus is on the types of constraints such a government faces.

This report introduces a simplified framework for the monetary system, along with the operating procedures that are associated with it. Some of the complications seen in real-world government finance are then added onto this simplified framework.

This report also acts as an introduction to some of the concepts used by Modern Monetary Theory, a school of thought within economics. Modern Monetary Theory emphasises the real limits of government action, as opposed to purely theoretical views about fiscal policy.